AF481152

FINDING AND IDENTIFYING FACTORS
Math Workbooks Grade 4
Children's Math Books

WHAT IS A FACTOR?

Factors are numbers we can multiply together to get another number.

EXAMPLE: The factors of 12, are 1, 2, 3, 4, 6 and 12.

$$1 \times 12 = 12$$
$$2 \times 6 = 12$$
$$3 \times 4 = 12$$

Each pair makes a total of 12.

PRIME FACTORIZATION TREE

Find the Prime Factors of the Numbers.

1) 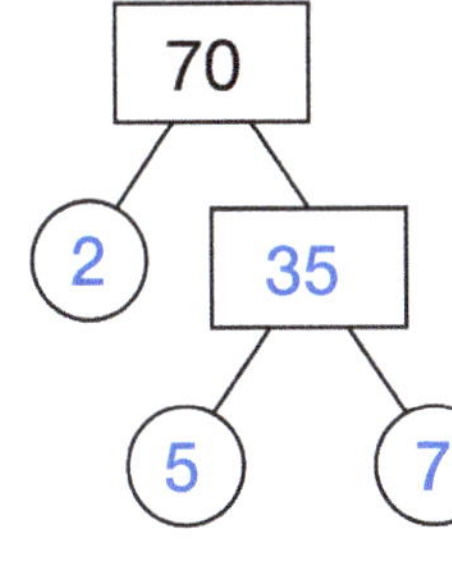

2) 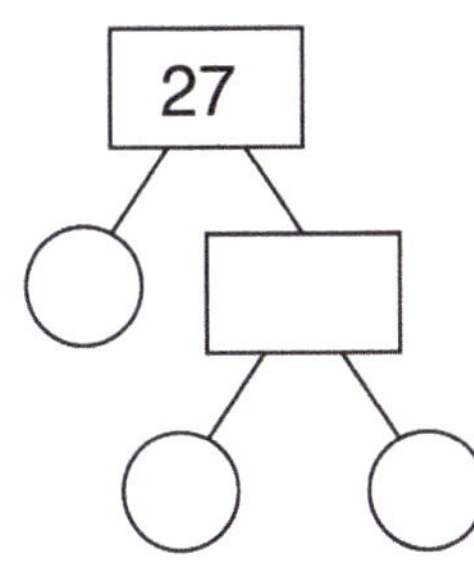

3) 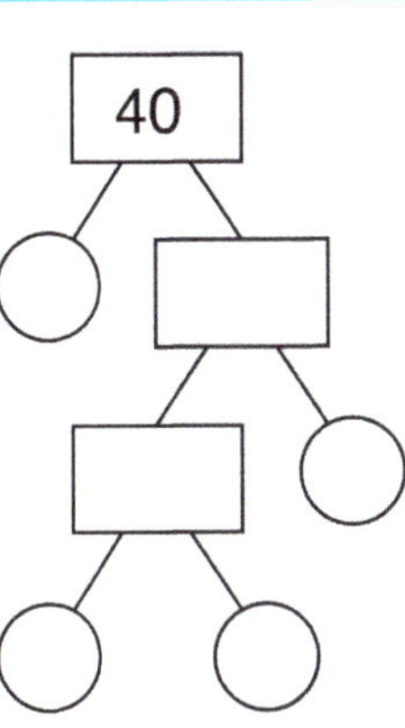

Prime Factors
2 x 5 x 7 = 70

Prime Factors
_ x _ x _ = 27

Prime Factors
_ x _ x _ x _ = 40

4) 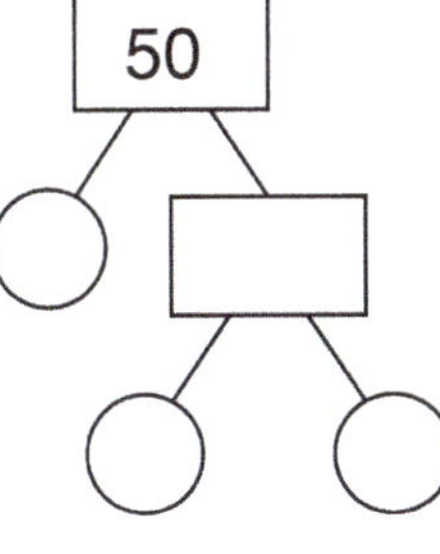

5) 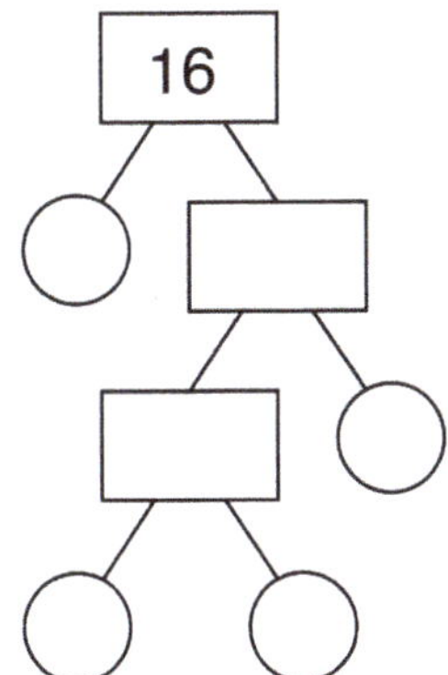

6) 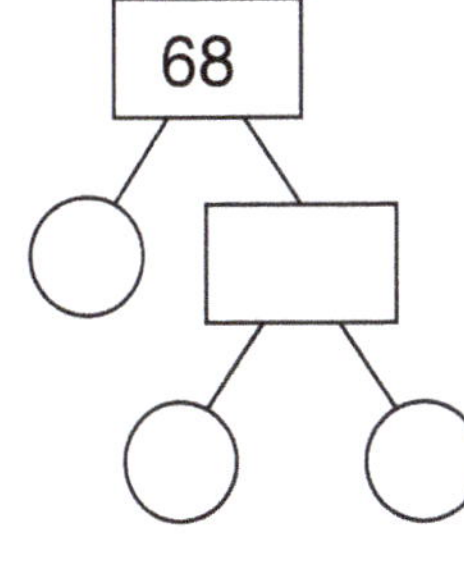

Prime Factors
_ x _ x _ = 50

Prime Factors
_ x _ x _ x _ = 16

Prime Factors
_ x _ x _ = 68

Find the Prime Factors of the Numbers.

1) 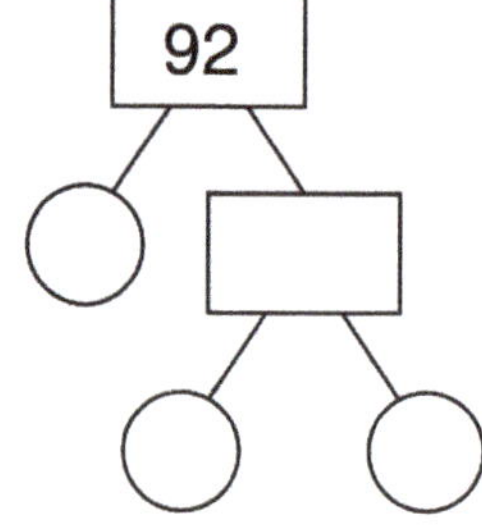

2) 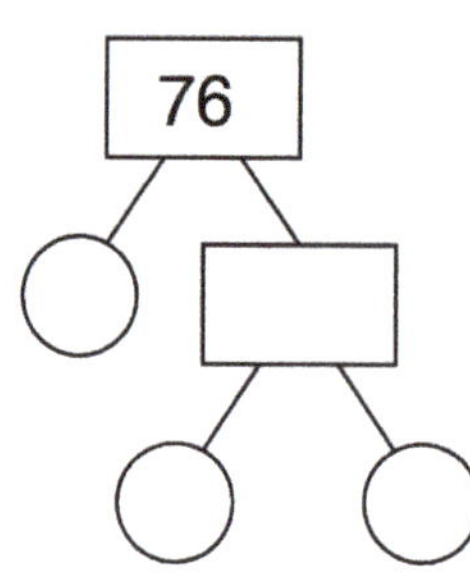

3) 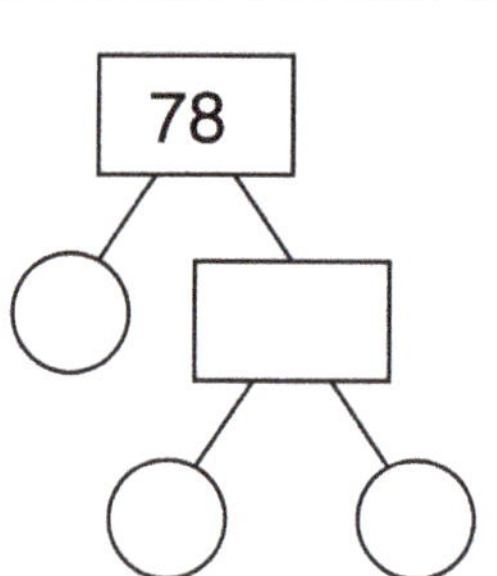

Prime Factors
_ x _ x _ = 92

Prime Factors
_ x _ x _ = 76

Prime Factors
_ x _ x _ = 78

4) 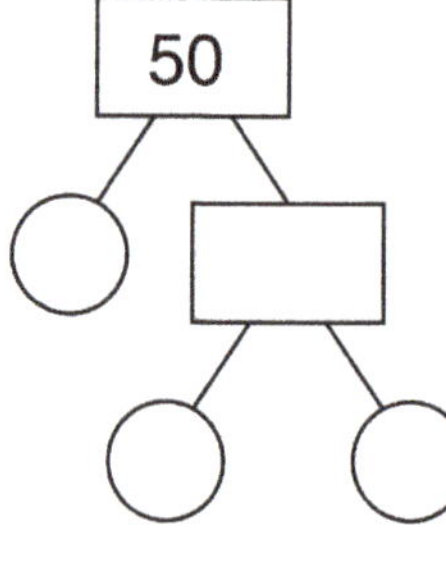

5) 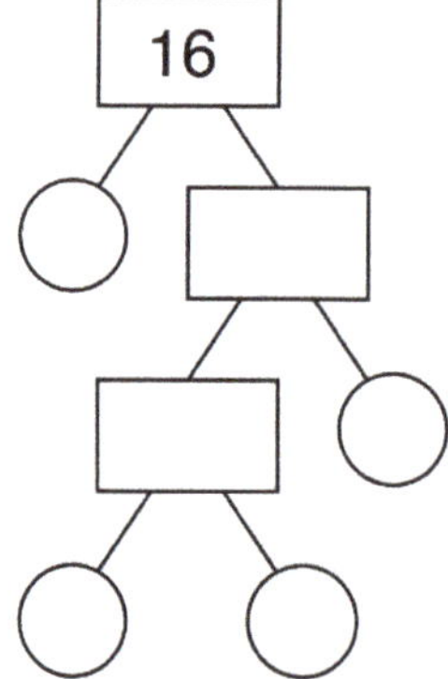

6) 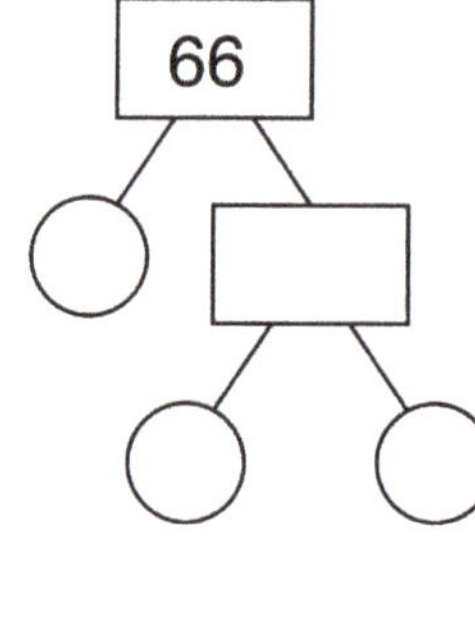

Prime Factors
_ x _ x _ = 50

Prime Factors
_ x _ x _ x _ = 16

Prime Factors
_ x _ x _ = 66

EXERCISE NO. 3

Find the Prime Factors of the Numbers.

1)
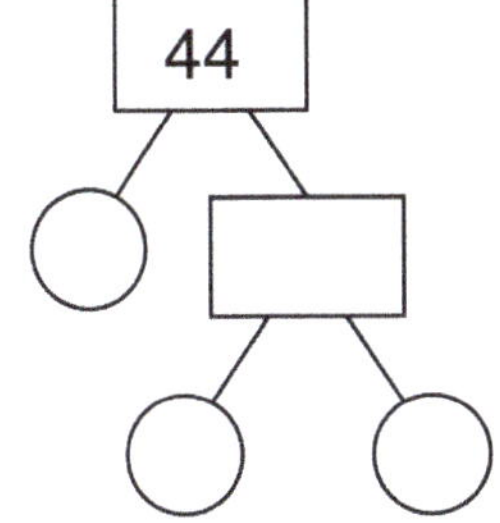

Prime Factors
_ x _ x _ = 44

2)
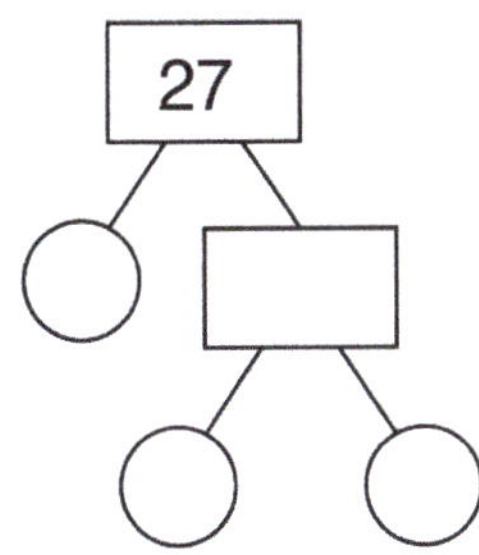

Prime Factors
_ x _ x _ = 27

3)
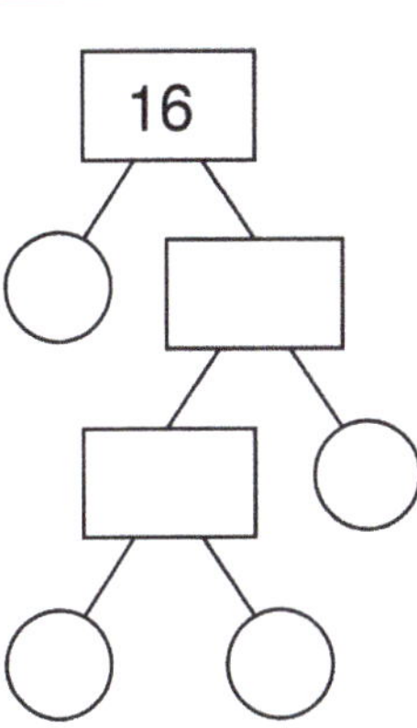

Prime Factors
_ x _ x _ x _ = 16

4)
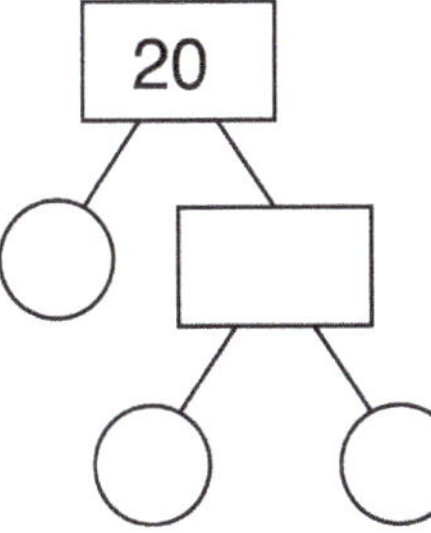

Prime Factors
_ x _ x _ = 20

5)
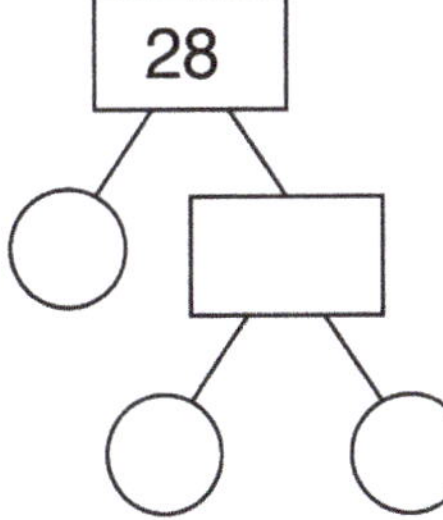

Prime Factors
_ x _ x _ = 28

6)
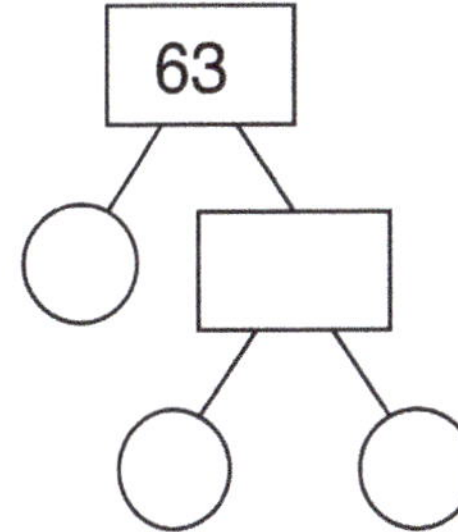

Prime Factors
_ x _ x _ = 63

Find the Prime Factors of the Numbers.

1) 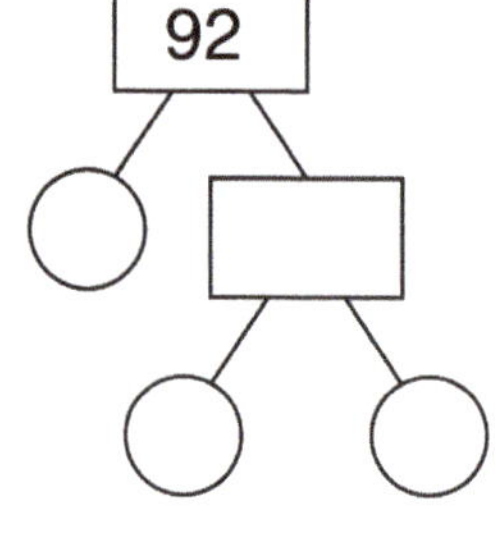

2) 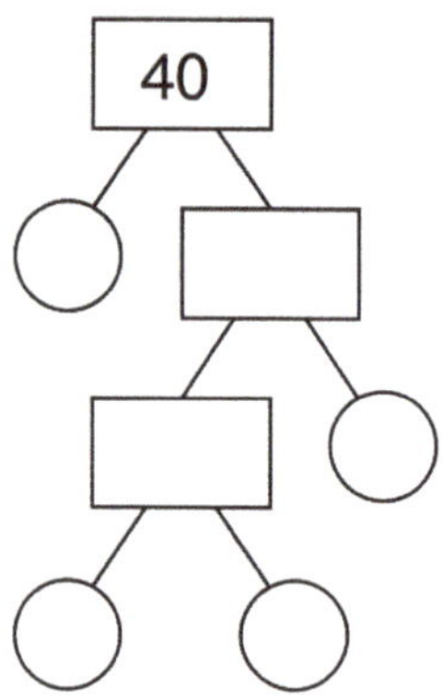

3) 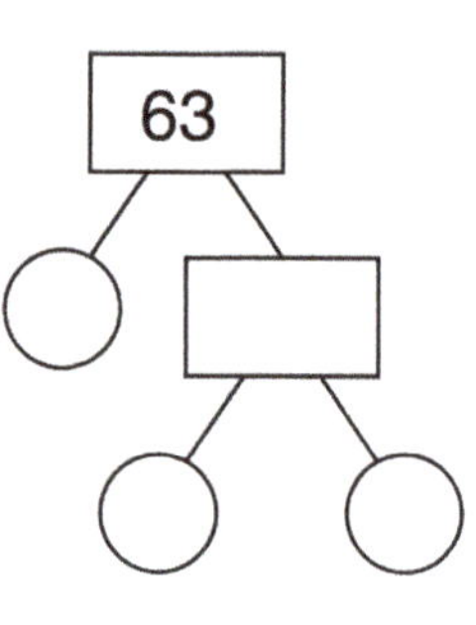

Prime Factors
_ x _ x _ = 92

Prime Factors
_ x _ x _ x _ = 40

Prime Factors
_ x _ x _ = 63

4) 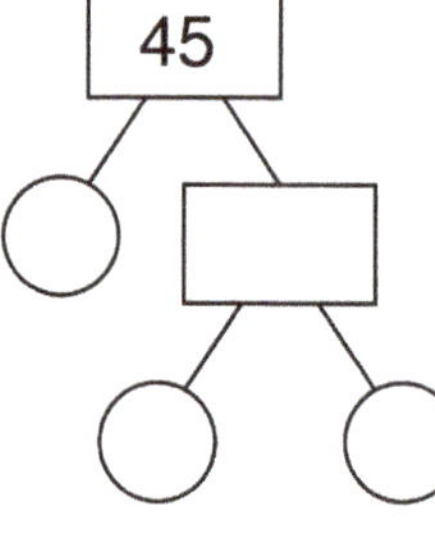

5) 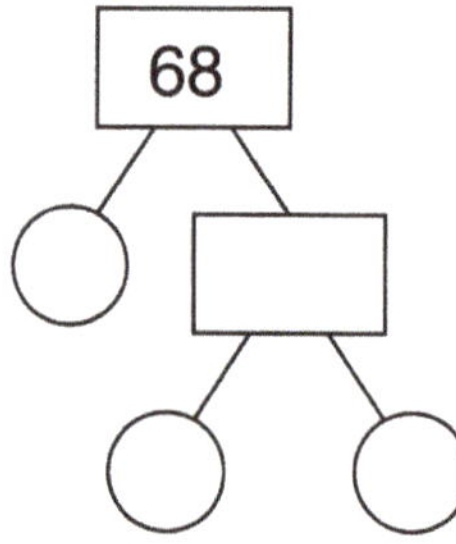

6) 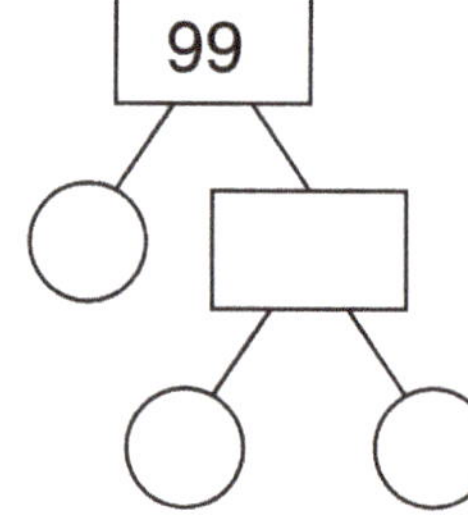

Prime Factors
_ x _ x _ = 45

Prime Factors
_ x _ x _ = 68

Prime Factors
_ x _ x _ = 99

Find the Prime Factors of the Numbers.

1) 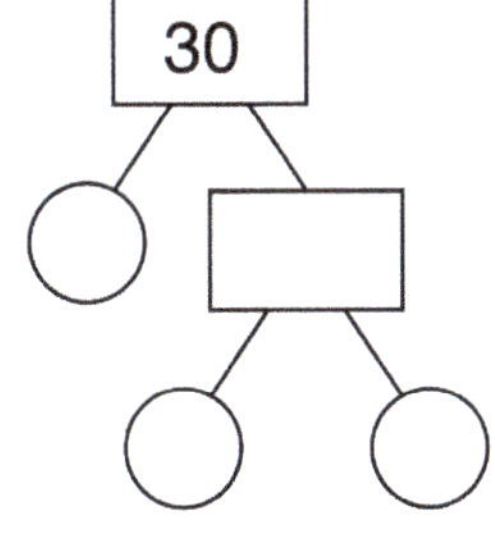

2) 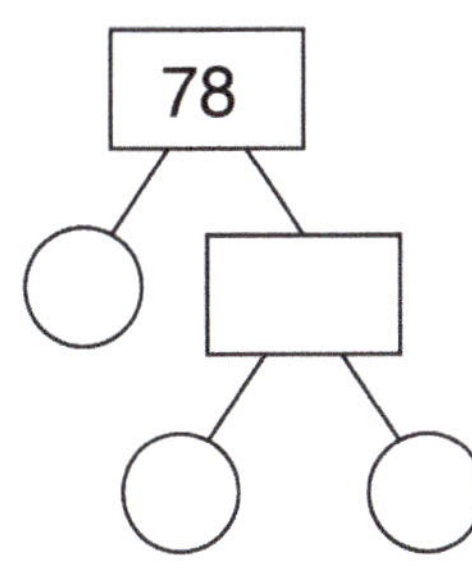

3) 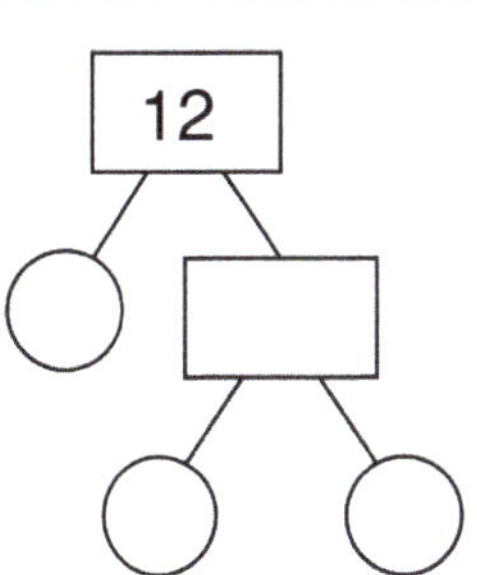

Prime Factors
_ x _ x _ = 30

Prime Factors
_ x _ x _ = 78

Prime Factors
_ x _ x _ = 12

---

4) 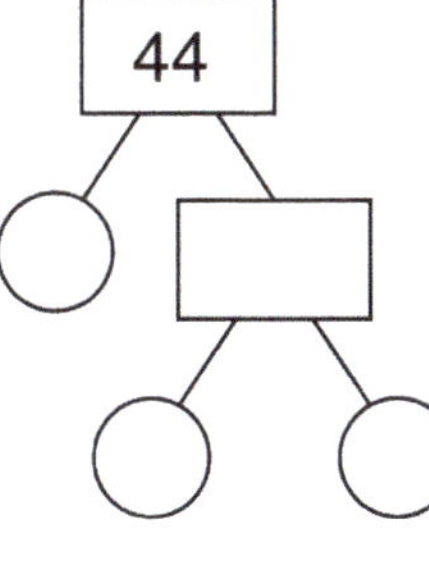

5) 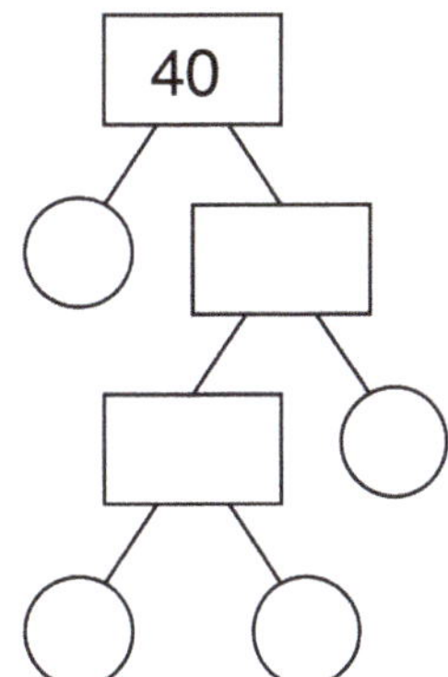

6) 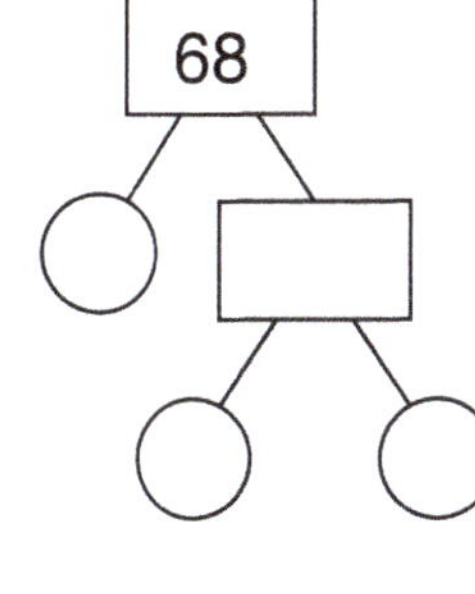

Prime Factors
_ x _ x _ = 44

Prime Factors
_ x _ x _ x _ = 40

Prime Factors
_ x _ x _ = 68

Find the Prime Factors of the Numbers.

1) 63

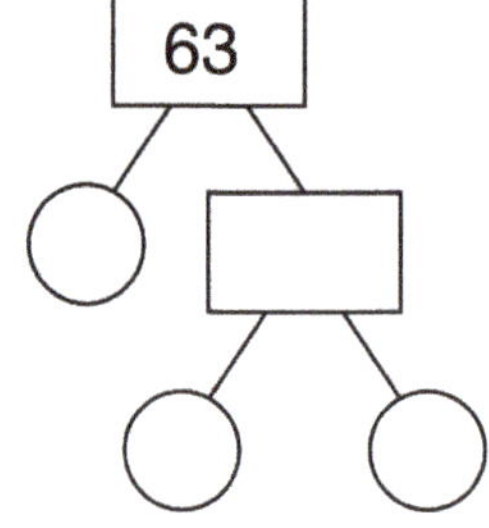

Prime Factors
_ x _ x _ = 63

2) 42

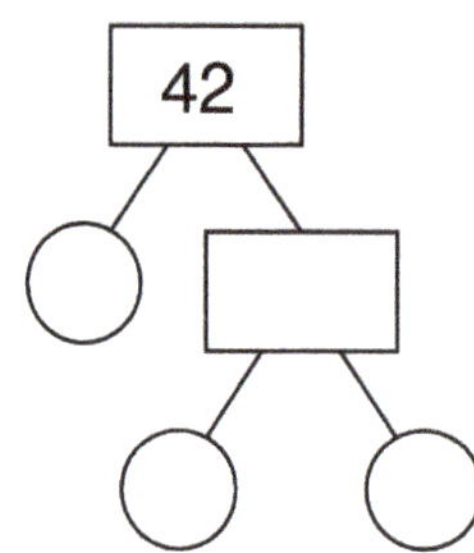

Prime Factors
_ x _ x _ = 42

3) 99

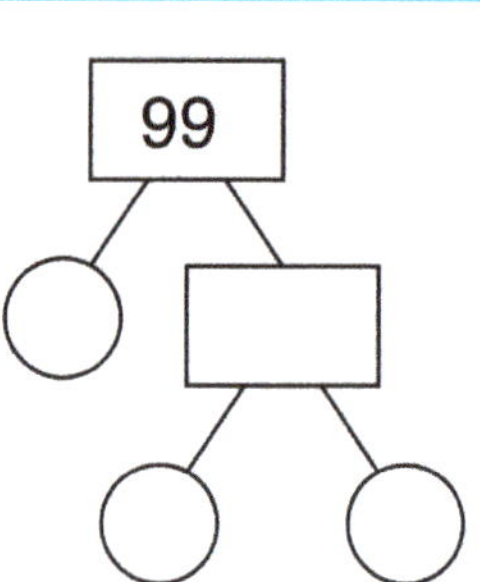

Prime Factors
_ x _ x _ = 99

4) 50

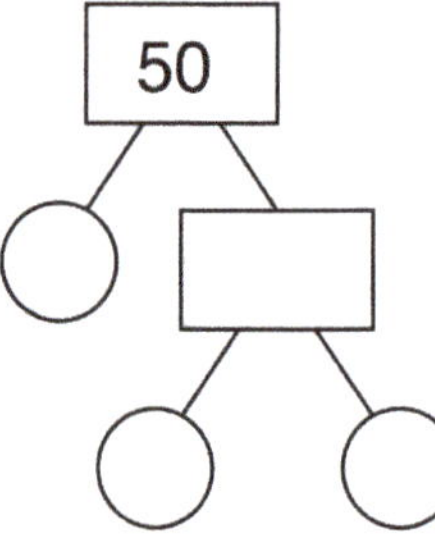

Prime Factors
_ x _ x _ = 50

5) 30

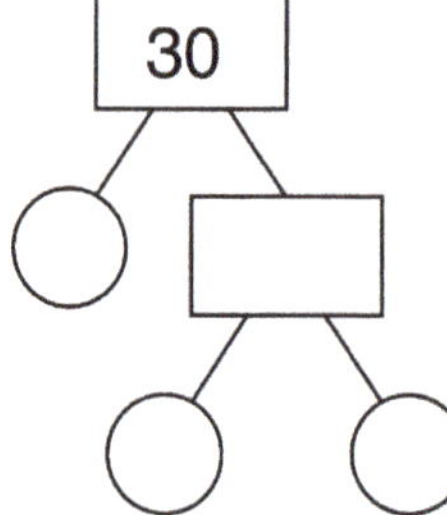

Prime Factors
_ x _ x _ = 30

6) 66

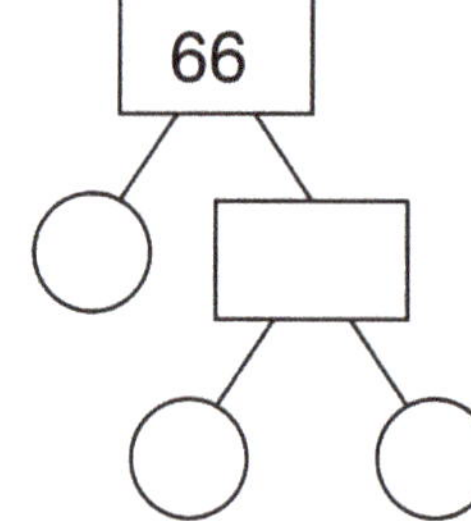

Prime Factors
_ x _ x _ = 66

EXERCISE NO. 7

Find the Prime Factors of the Numbers.

1) 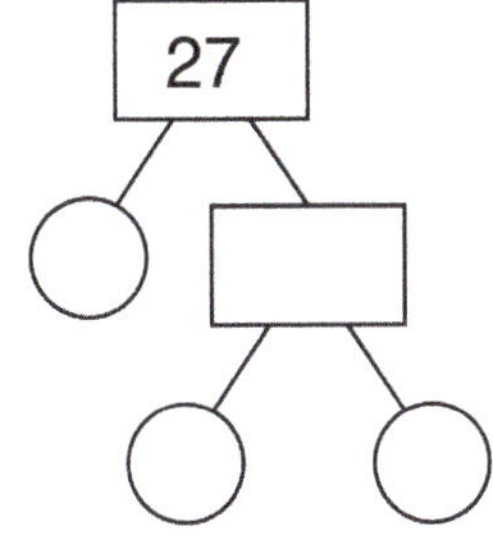

Prime Factors
_ x _ x _ = 27

2) 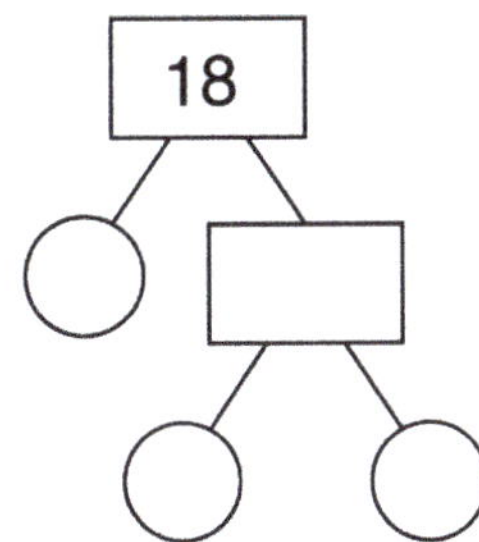

Prime Factors
_ x _ x _ = 18

3) 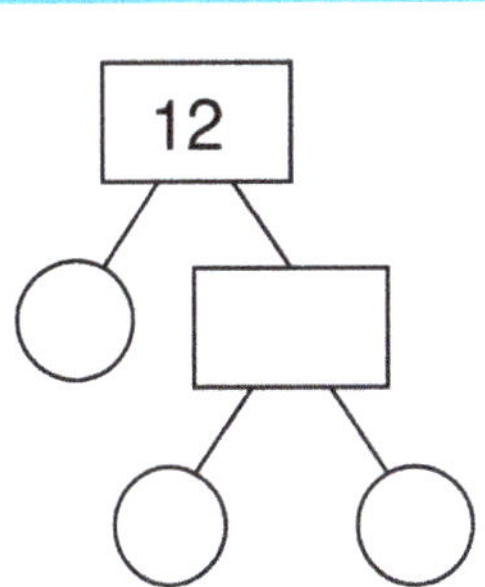

Prime Factors
_ x _ x _ = 12

4) 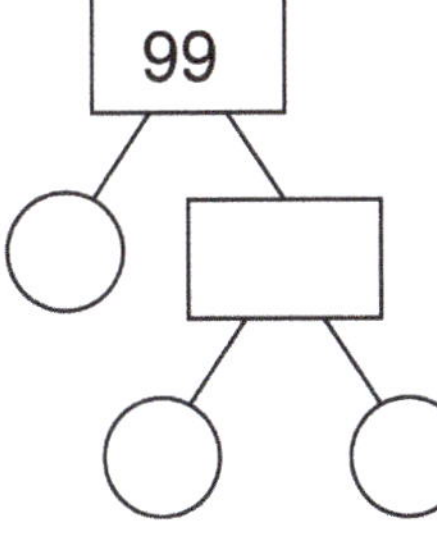

Prime Factors
_ x _ x _ = 99

5) 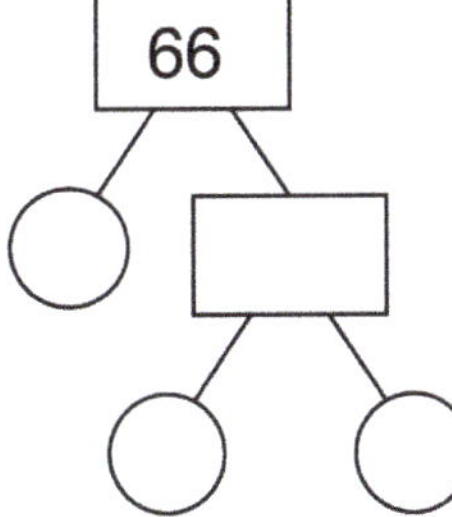

Prime Factors
_ x _ x _ = 66

6) 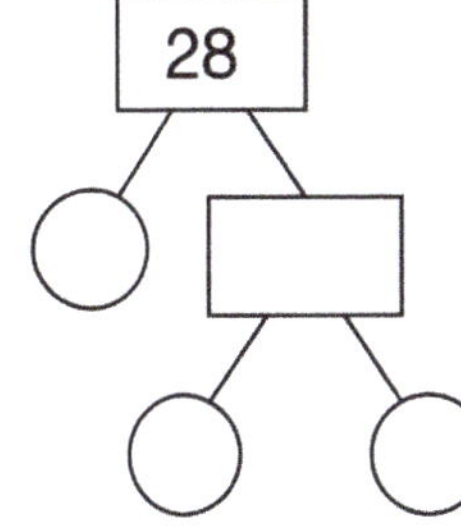

Prime Factors
_ x _ x _ = 28

Find the Prime Factors of the Numbers.

1)

45

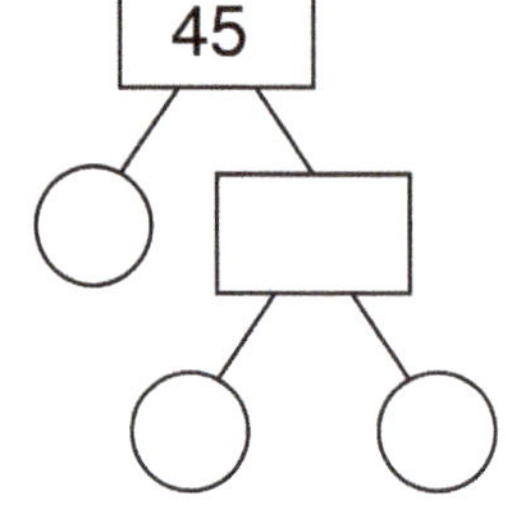

Prime Factors

_ x _ x _ = 45

2)

92

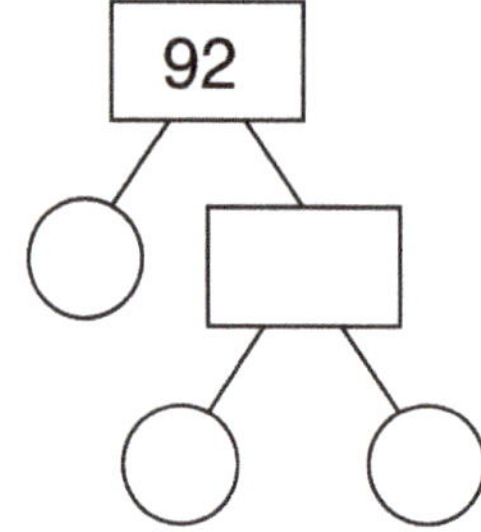

Prime Factors

_ x _ x _ = 92

3)

78

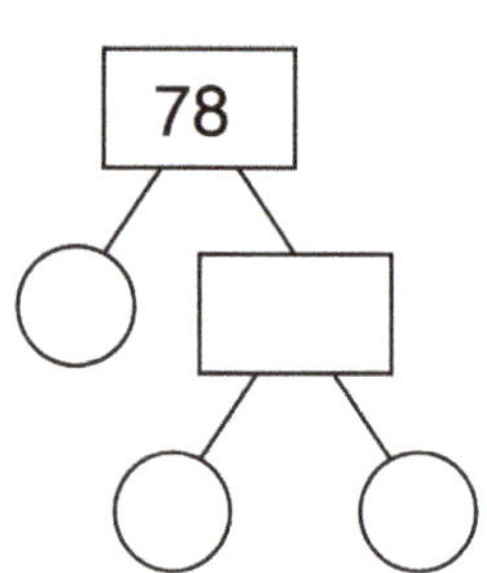

Prime Factors

_ x _ x _ = 78

4)

20

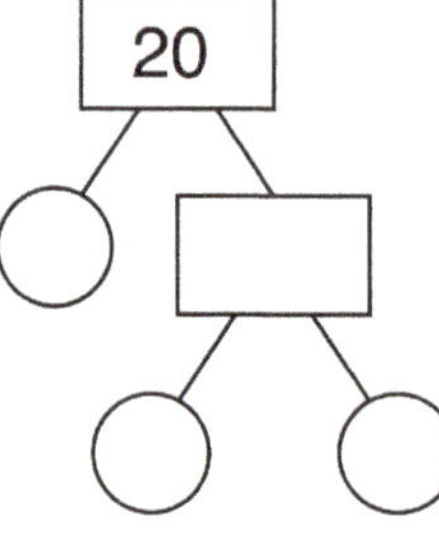

Prime Factors

_ x _ x _ = 20

5)

44

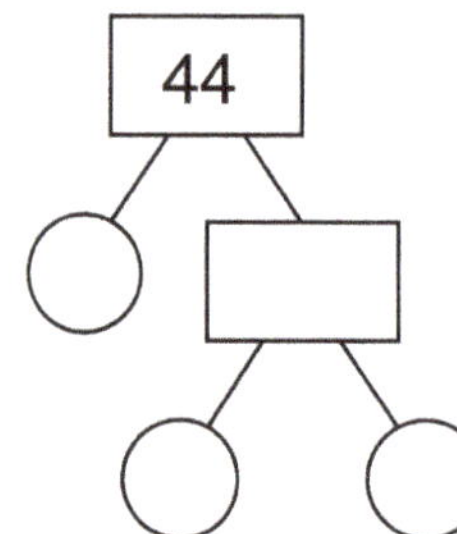

Prime Factors

_ x _ x _ = 44

6)

66

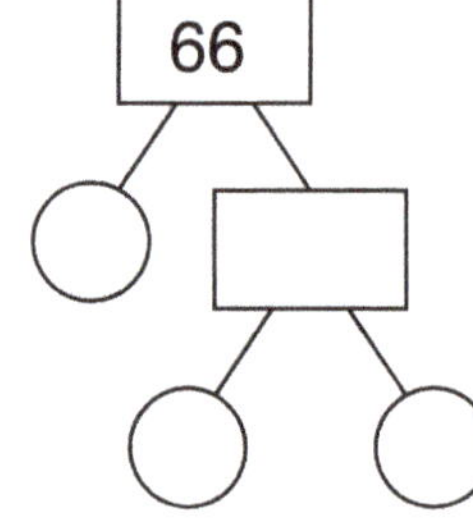

Prime Factors

_ x _ x _ = 66

Find the Prime Factors of the Numbers.

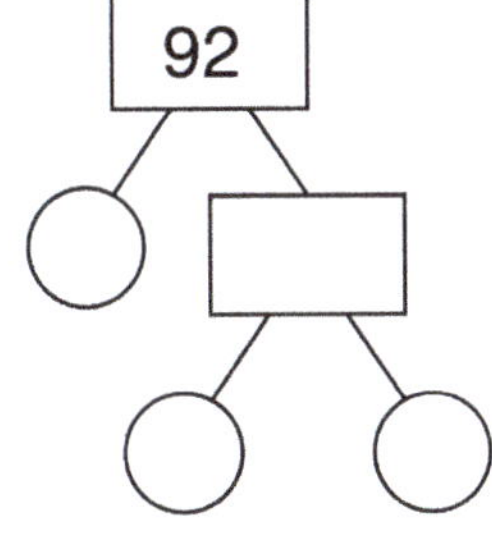

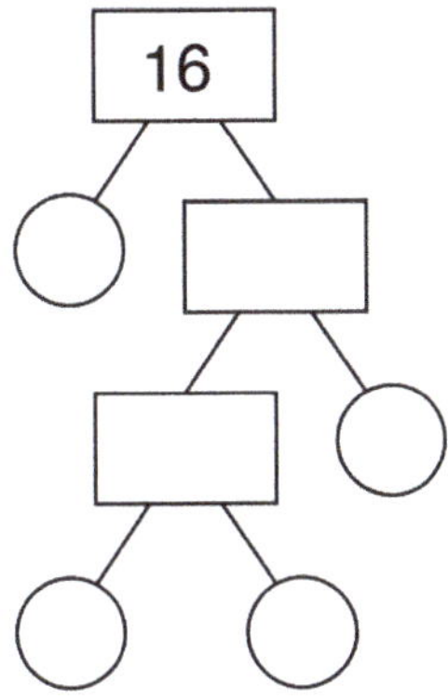

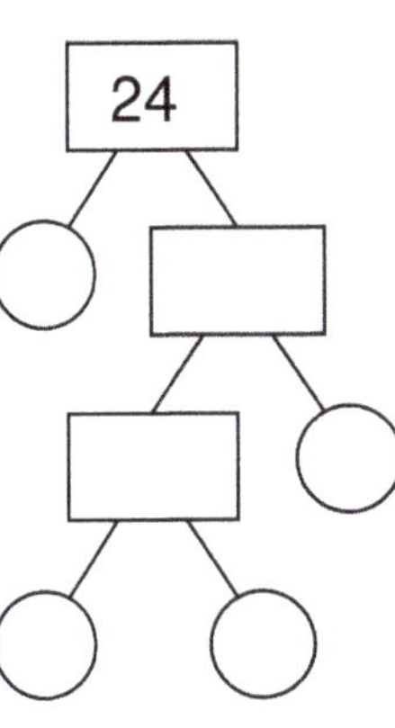

Prime Factors

_ x _ x _ = 92

Prime Factors

_ x _ x _ x _ = 16

Prime Factors

_ x _ x _ x _ = 24

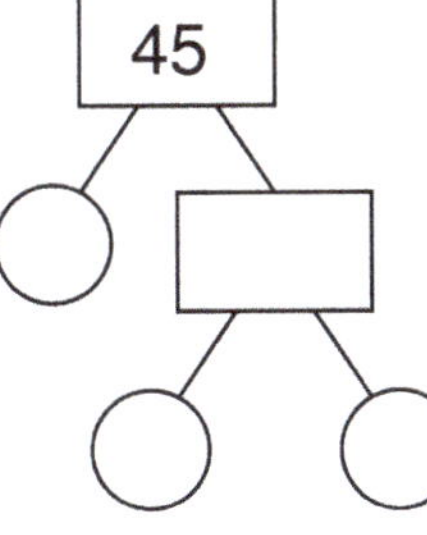

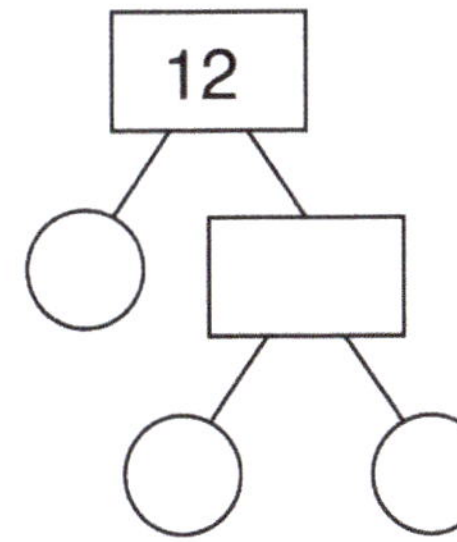

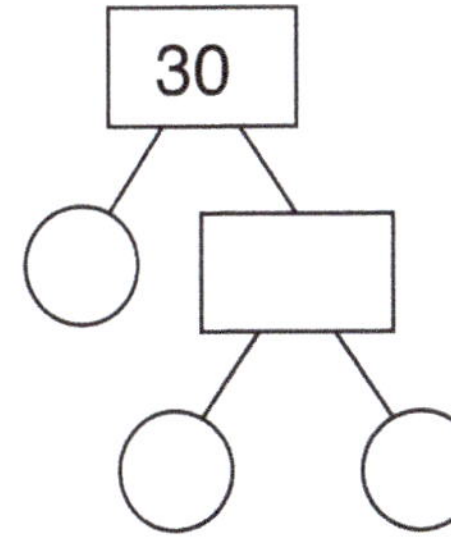

Prime Factors

_ x _ x _ = 45

Prime Factors

_ x _ x _ = 12

Prime Factors

_ x _ x _ = 30

EXERCISE NO. 10

Find the Prime Factors of the Numbers.

1)
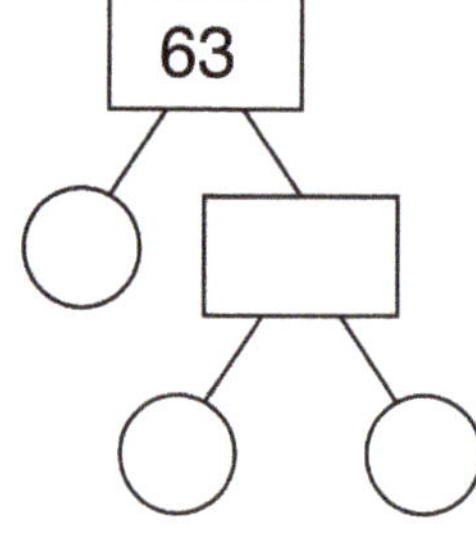

Prime Factors
_ x _ x _ = 63

2)
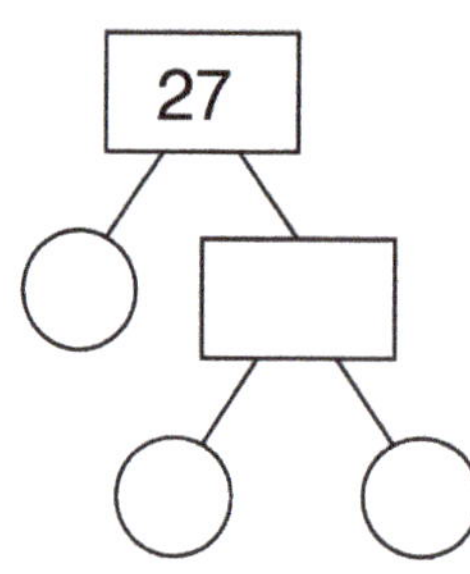

Prime Factors
_ x _ x _ = 27

3)
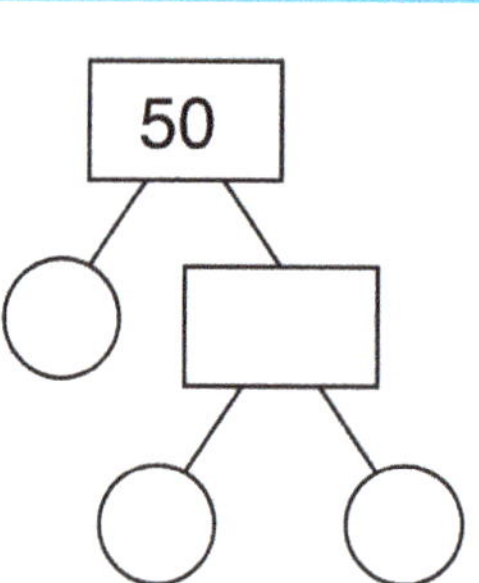

Prime Factors
_ x _ x _ = 50

4)
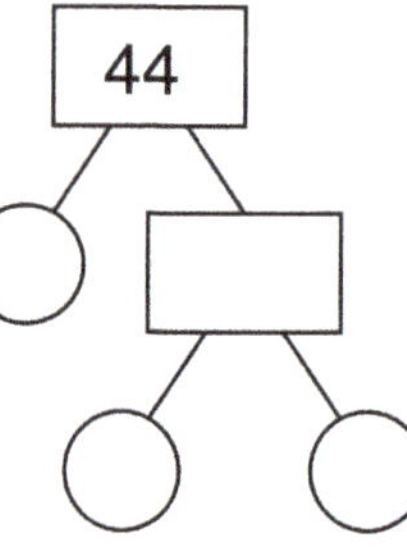

Prime Factors
_ x _ x _ = 44

5)
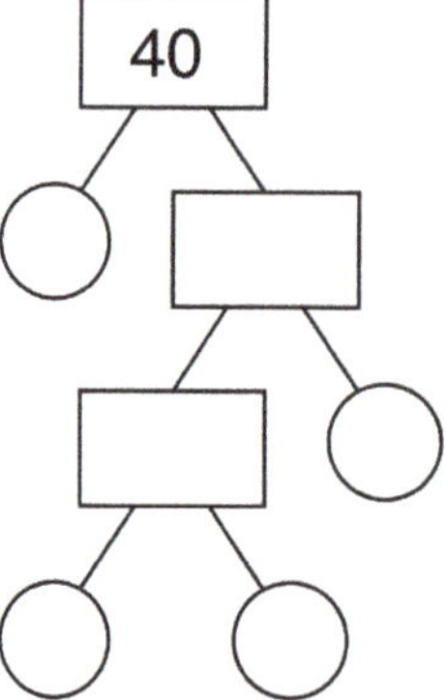

Prime Factors
_ x _ x _ x _ = 40

6)
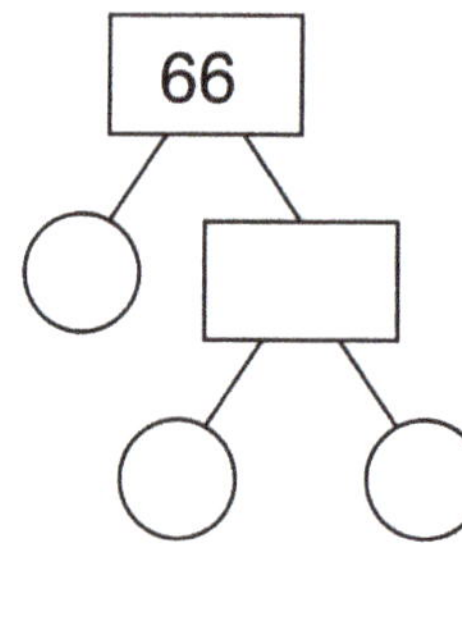

Prime Factors
_ x _ x _ = 66

Find the Prime Factors of the Numbers.

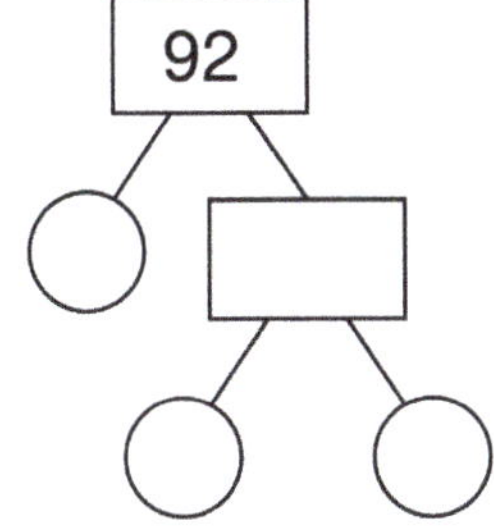

1) 92

Prime Factors
_ x _ x _ = 92

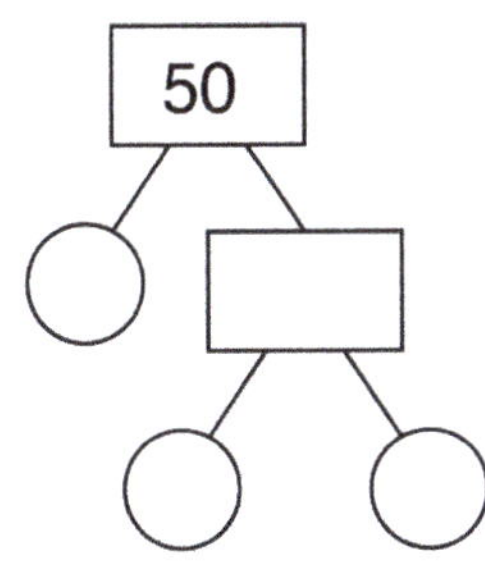

2) 50

Prime Factors
_ x _ x _ = 50

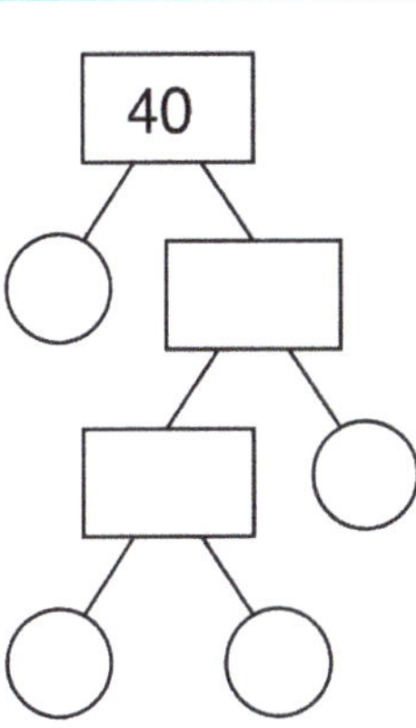

3) 40

Prime Factors
_ x _ x _ x _ = 40

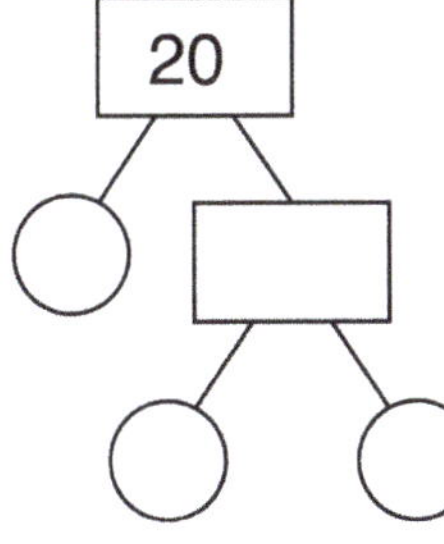

4) 20

Prime Factors
_ x _ x _ = 20

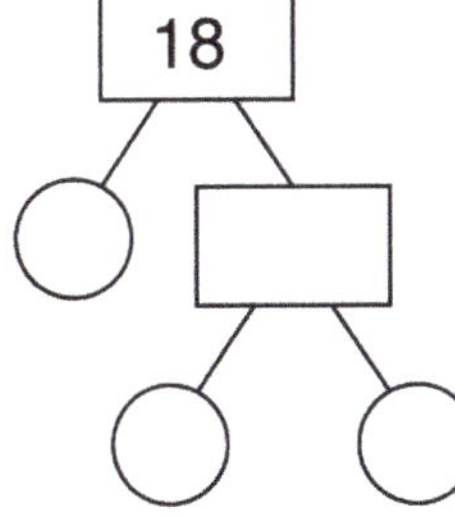

5) 18

Prime Factors
_ x _ x _ = 18

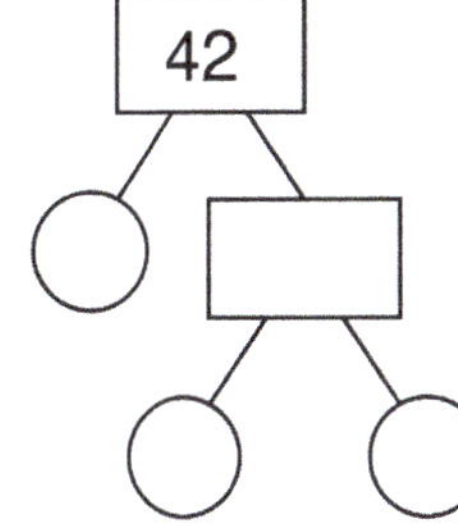

6) 42

Prime Factors
_ x _ x _ = 42

Find the Prime Factors of the Numbers.

1)

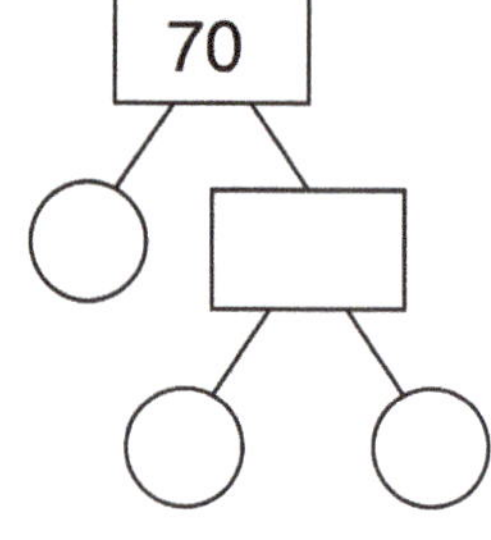

70

Prime Factors

_ x _ x _ = 70

2)

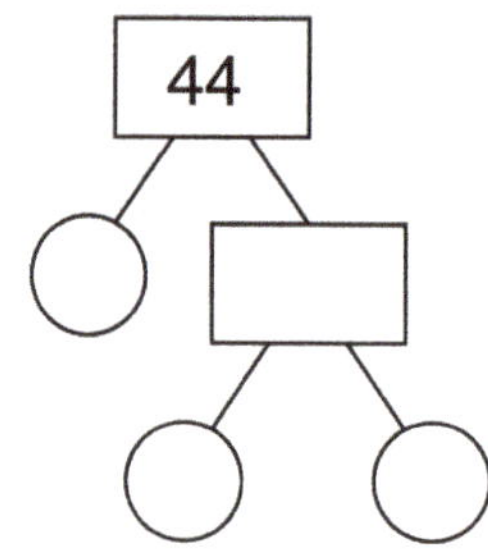

44

Prime Factors

_ x _ x _ = 44

3)

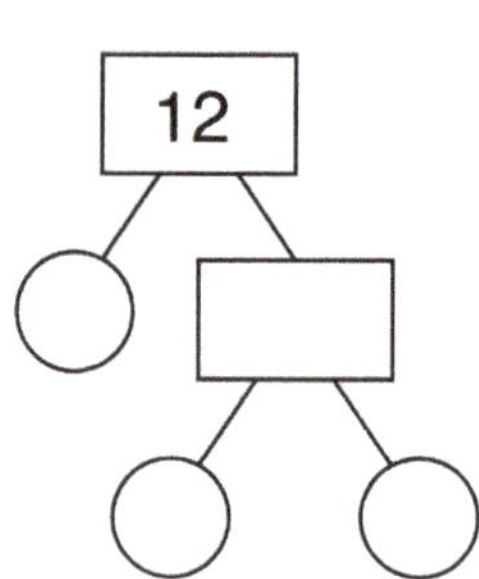

12

Prime Factors

_ x _ x _ = 12

4)

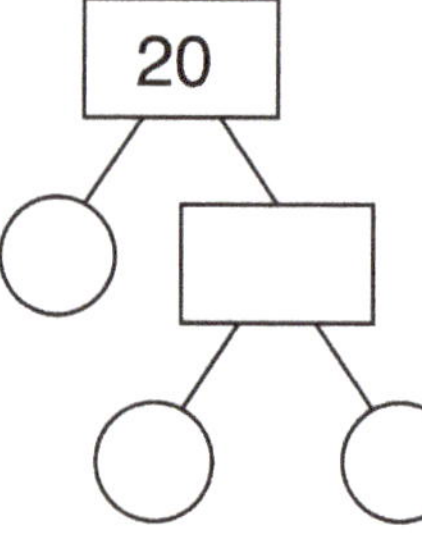

20

Prime Factors

_ x _ x _ = 20

5)

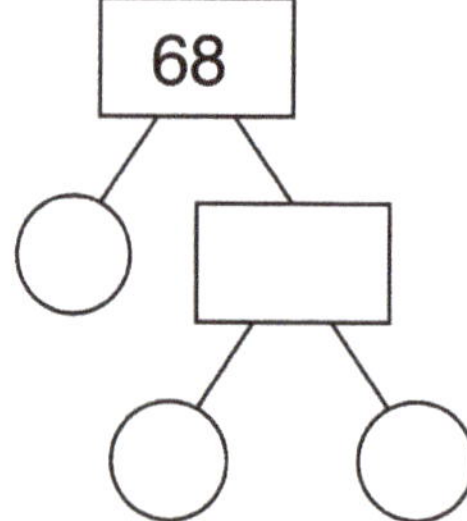

68

Prime Factors

_ x _ x _ = 68

6)

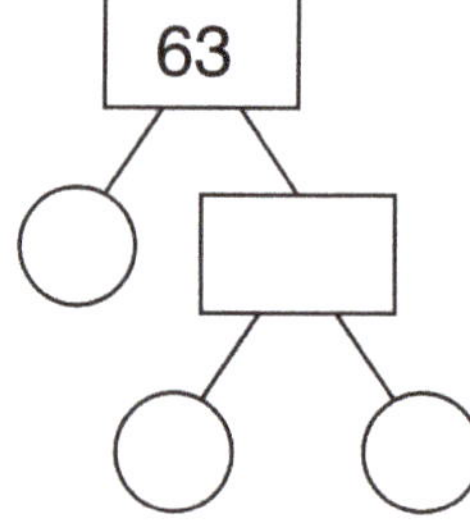

63

Prime Factors

_ x _ x _ = 63

Find the Prime Factors of the Numbers.

1) 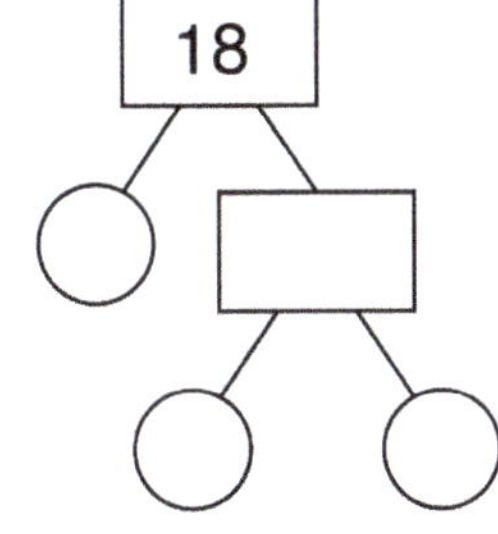

18

2) 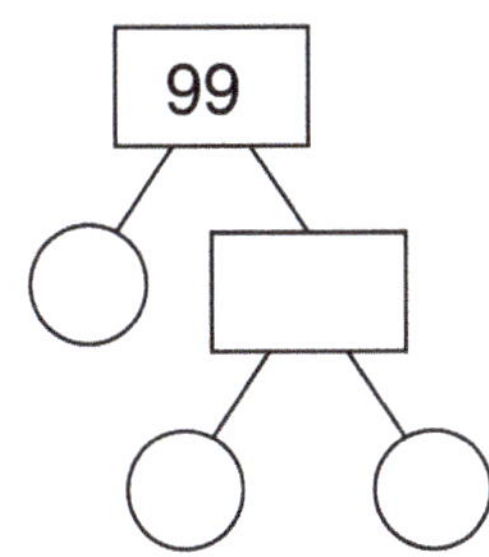

99

3) 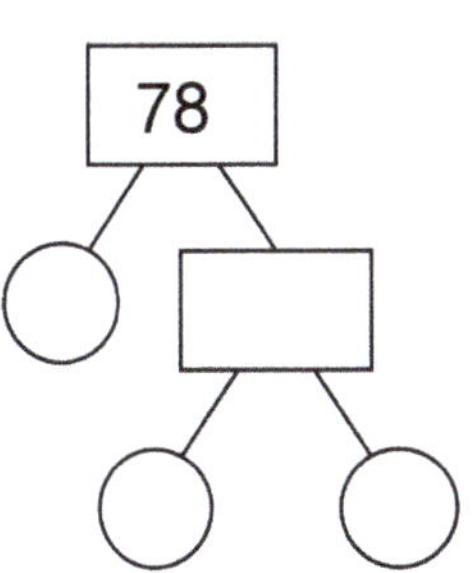

78

Prime Factors
_ x _ x _ = 18

Prime Factors
_ x _ x _ = 99

Prime Factors
_ x _ x _ = 78

---

4) 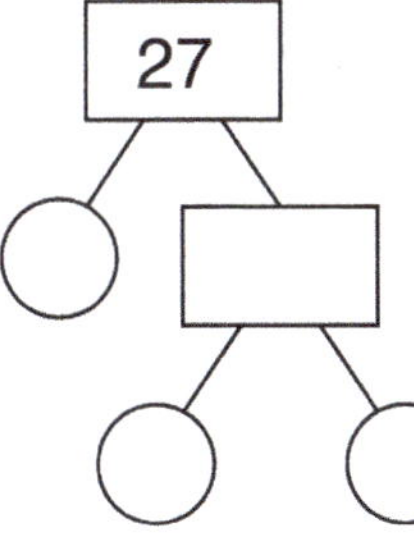

27

5) 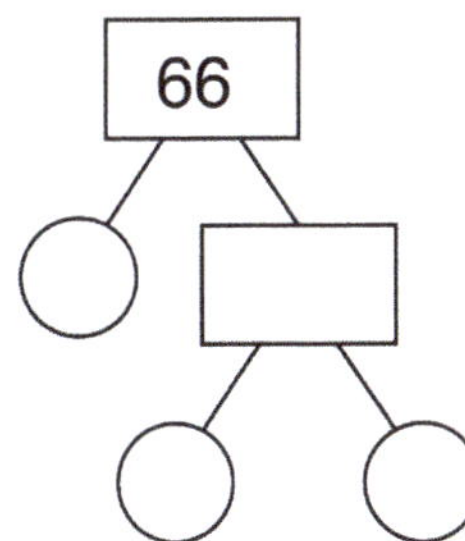

66

6) 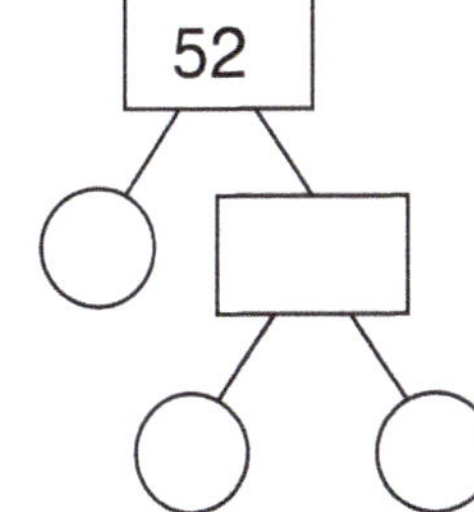

52

Prime Factors
_ x _ x _ = 27

Prime Factors
_ x _ x _ = 66

Prime Factors
_ x _ x _ = 52

Find the Prime Factors of the Numbers.

1)
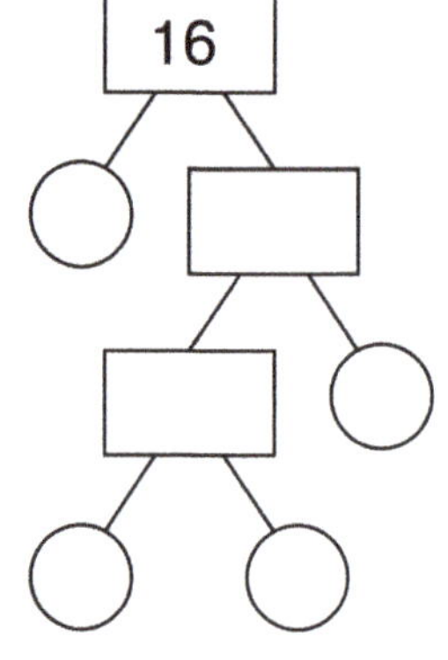

2)
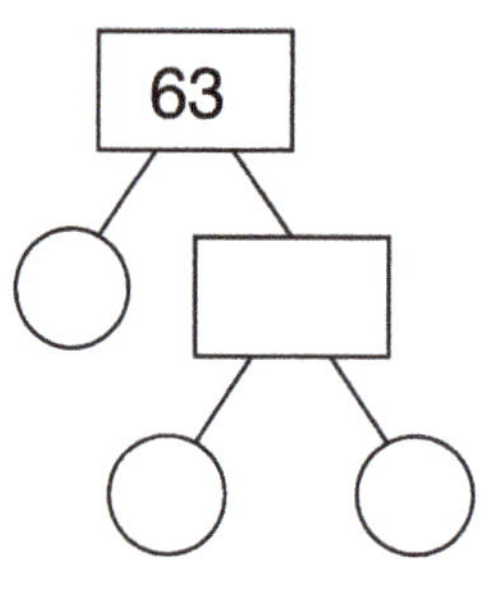

3)
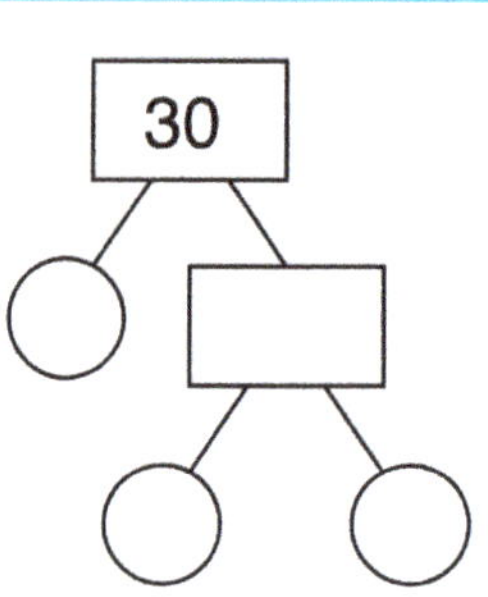

Prime Factors
_ x _ x _ x _ = 16

Prime Factors
_ x _ x _ = 63

Prime Factors
_ x _ x _ = 30

---

4)
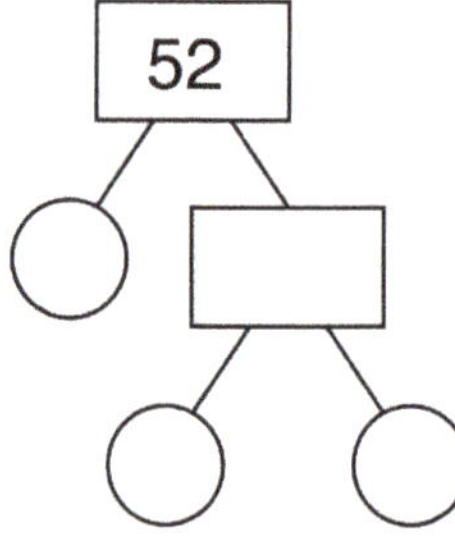

5)
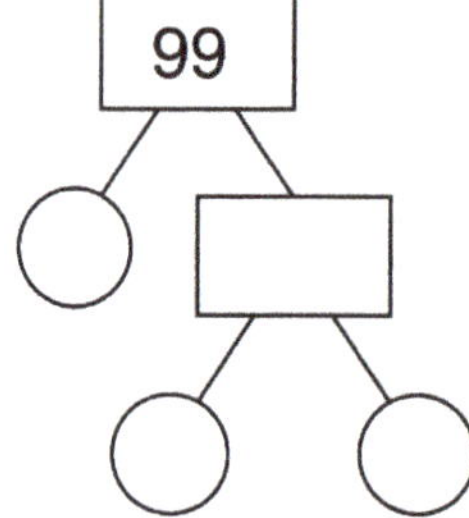

6)
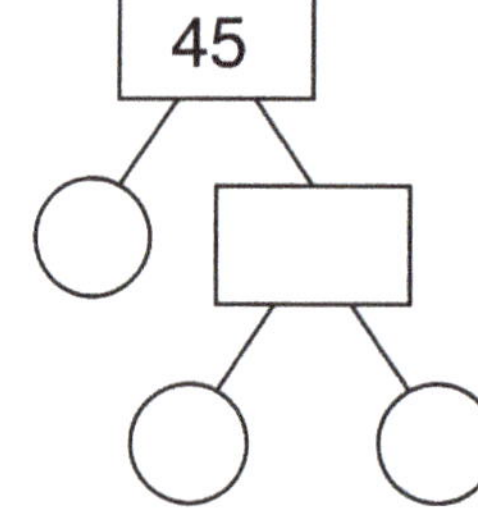

Prime Factors
_ x _ x _ = 52

Prime Factors
_ x _ x _ = 99

Prime Factors
_ x _ x _ = 45

Find the Prime Factors of the Numbers.

1)

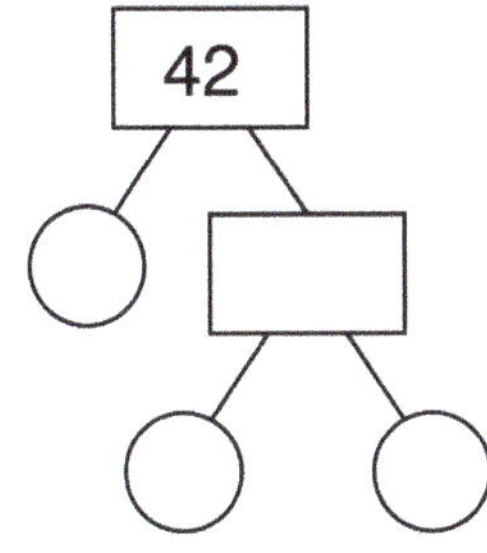

Prime Factors
_ x _ x _ = 42

2)

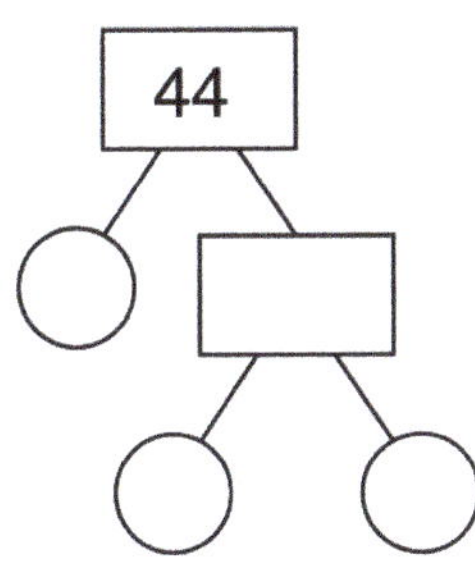

Prime Factors
_ x _ x _ = 44

3)

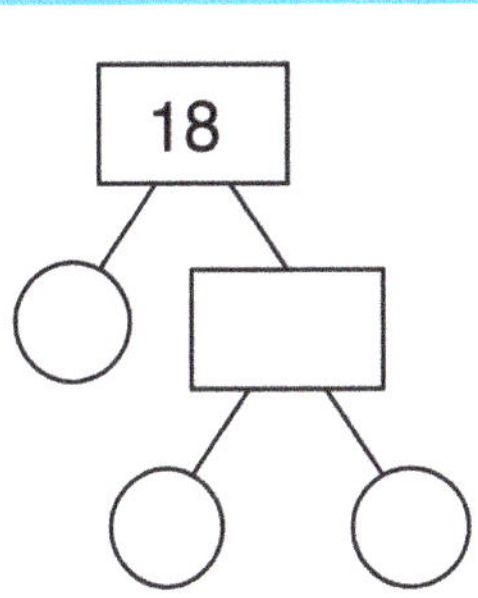

Prime Factors
_ x _ x _ = 18

4)

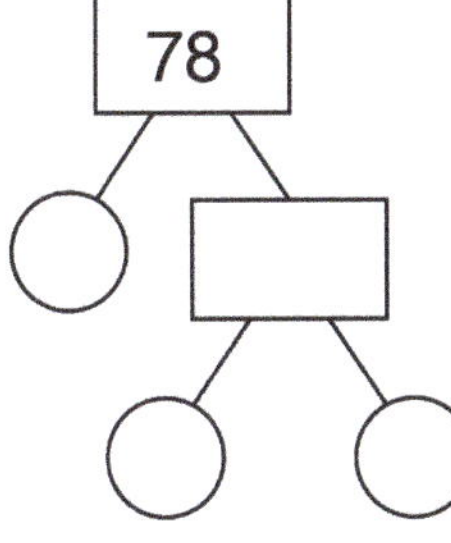

Prime Factors
_ x _ x _ = 78

5)

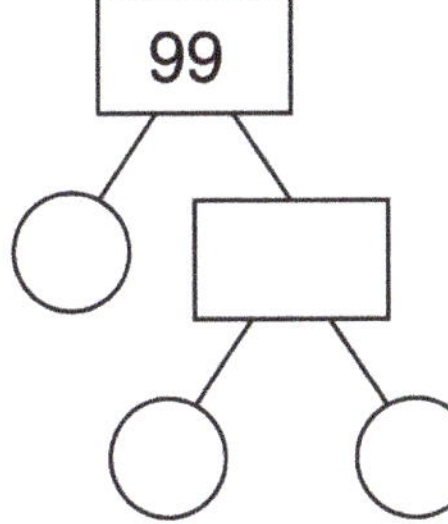

Prime Factors
_ x _ x _ = 99

6)

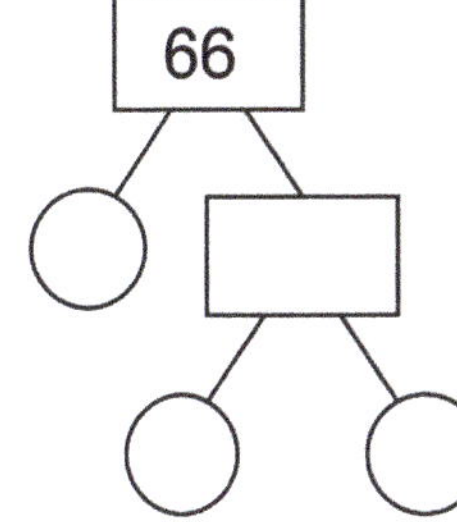

Prime Factors
_ x _ x _ = 66

Find the Prime Factors of the Numbers.

1)
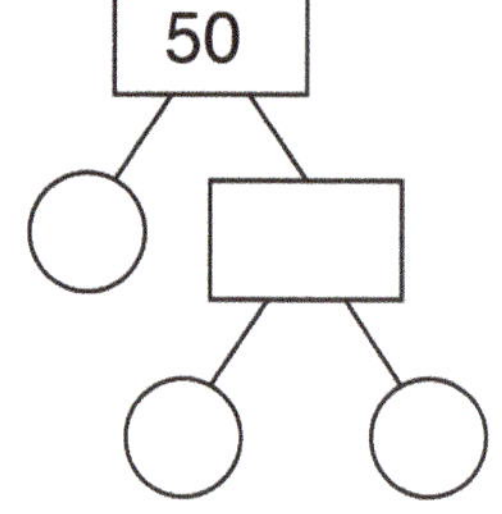
50

Prime Factors
_ x _ x _ = 50

2)
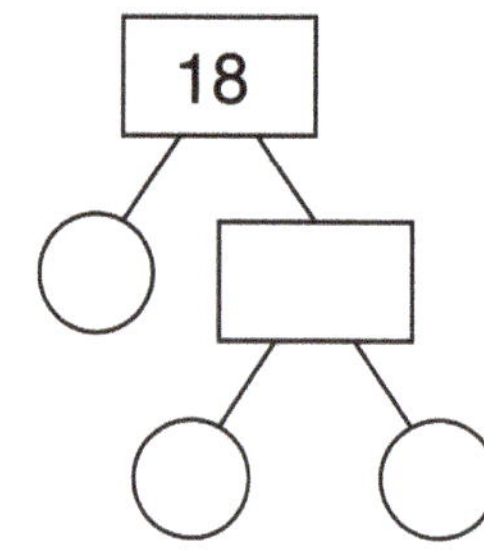
18

Prime Factors
_ x _ x _ = 18

3)
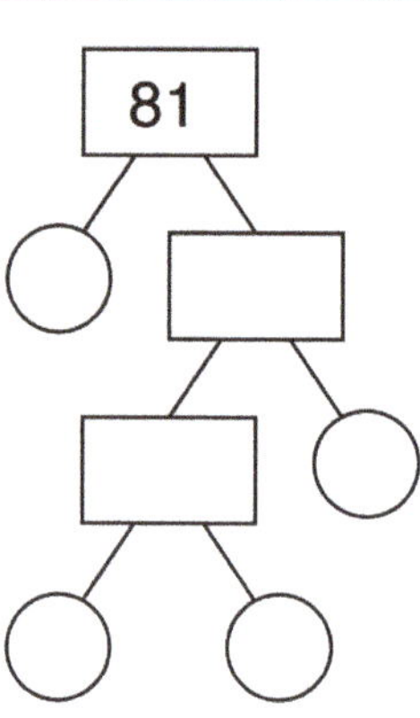
81

Prime Factors
_ x _ x _ x _ = 81

4)
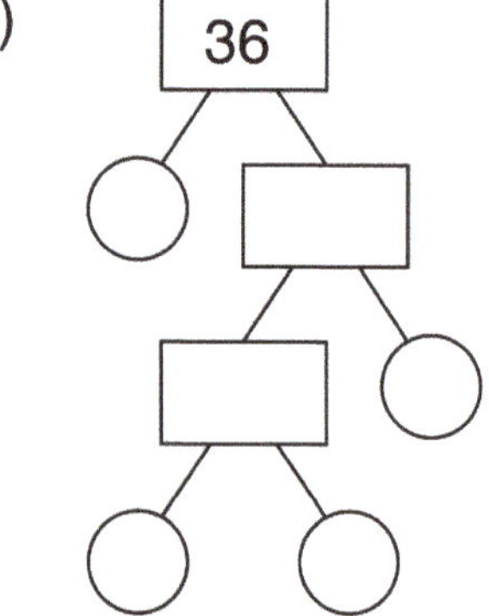
36

Prime Factors
_ x _ x _ x _ = 36

5)
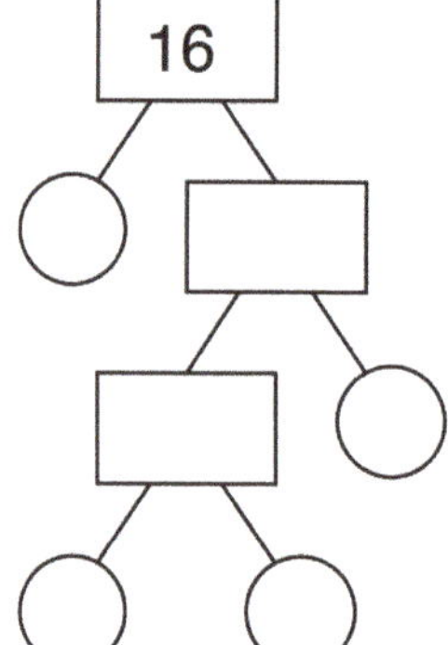
16

Prime Factors
_ x _ x _ x _ = 16

6)
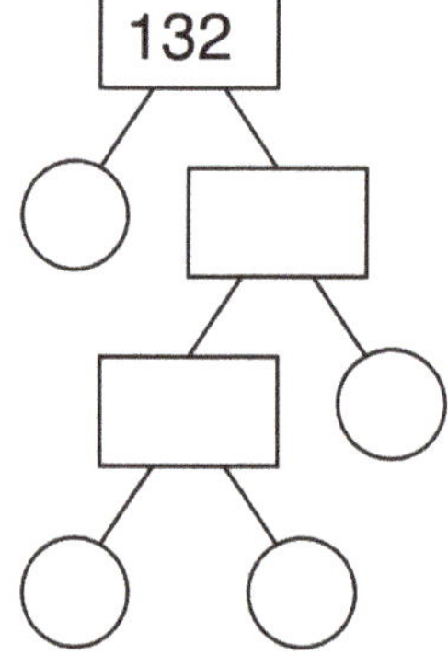
132

Prime Factors
_ x _ x _ x _ = 132

Find the Prime Factors of the Numbers.

1) 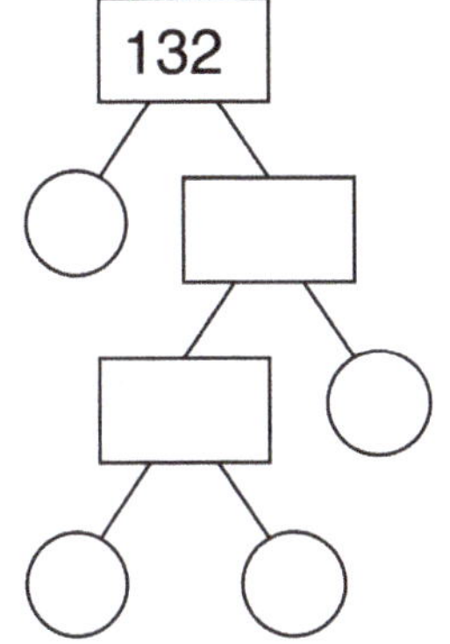

2) 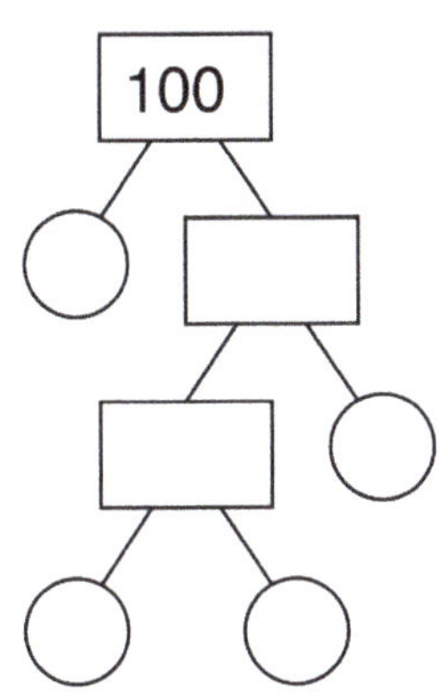

3) 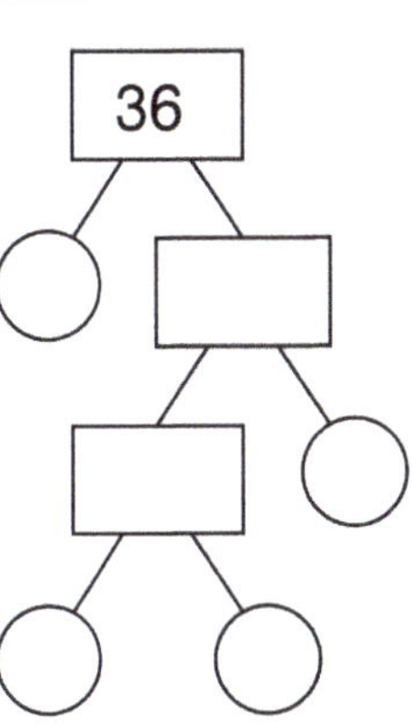

Prime Factors
_ x _ x _ x _ = 132

Prime Factors
_ x _ x _ x _ = 100

Prime Factors
_ x _ x _ x _ = 36

4) 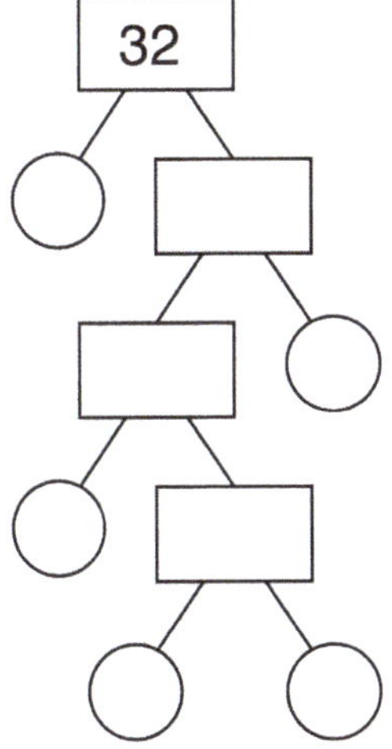

5) 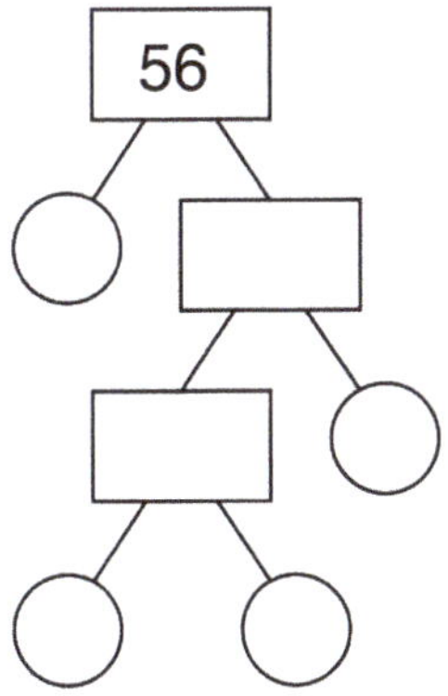

6) 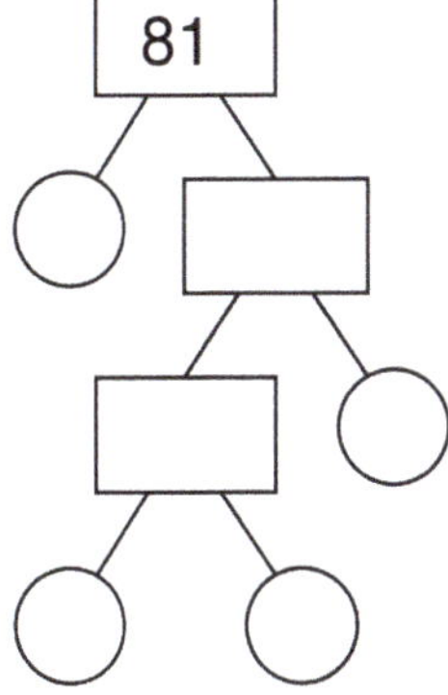

Prime Factors
_ x _ x _ x _ x _ = 32

Prime Factors
_ x _ x _ x _ = 56

Prime Factors
_ x _ x _ x _ = 81

Find the Prime Factors of the Numbers.

1) 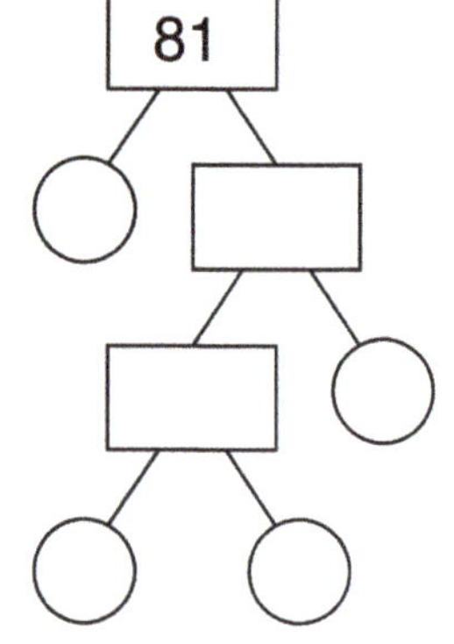

2) 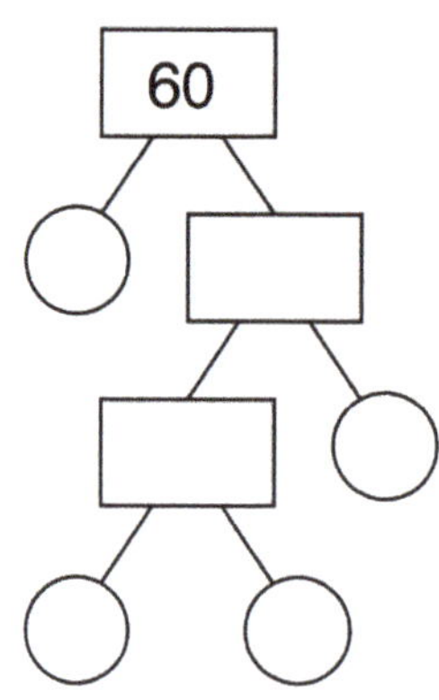

3) 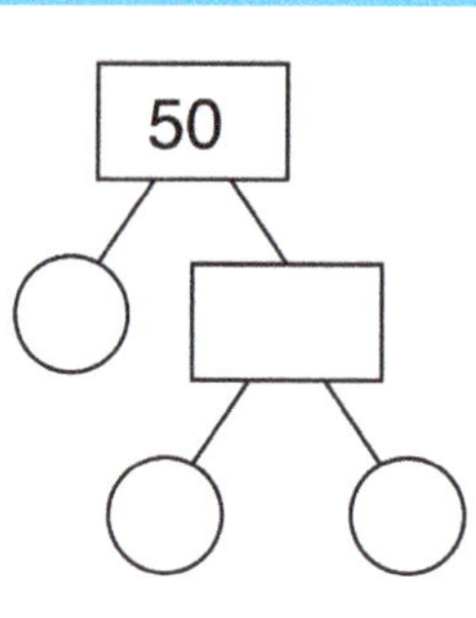

Prime Factors
_ x _ x _ x _ = 81

Prime Factors
_ x _ x _ x _ = 60

Prime Factors
_ x _ x _ = 50

4) 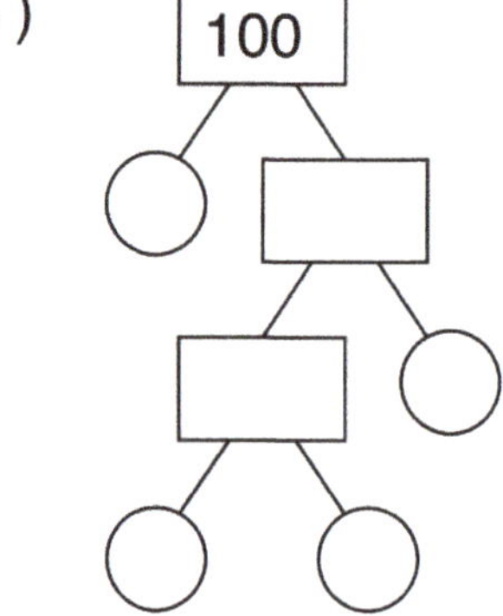

5) 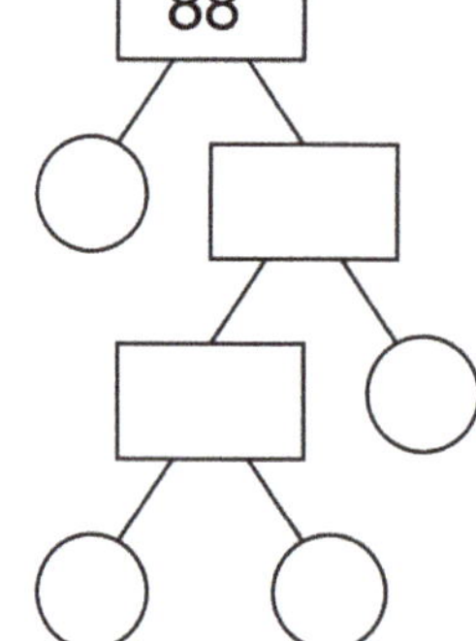

6) 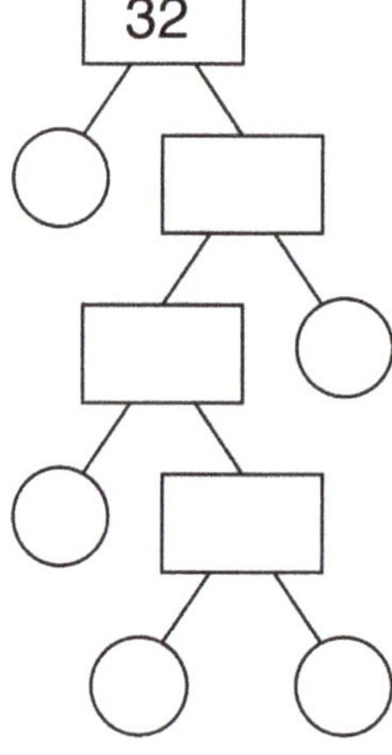

Prime Factors
_ x _ x _ x _ = 100

Prime Factors
_ x _ x _ x _ = 88

Prime Factors
_ x _ x _ x _ x _ = 32

Find the Prime Factors of the Numbers.

1) 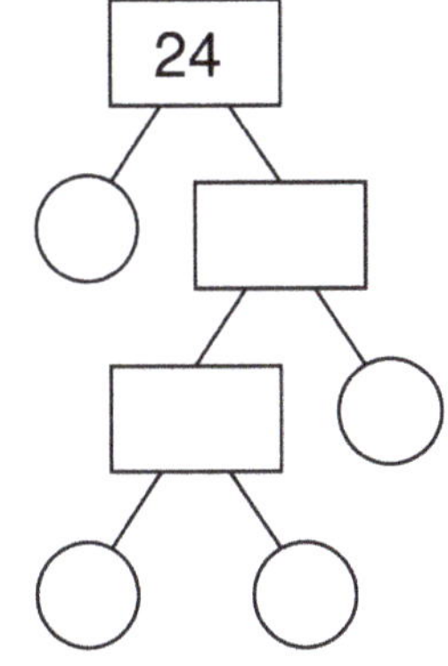

Prime Factors

_ x _ x _ x _ = 24

2) 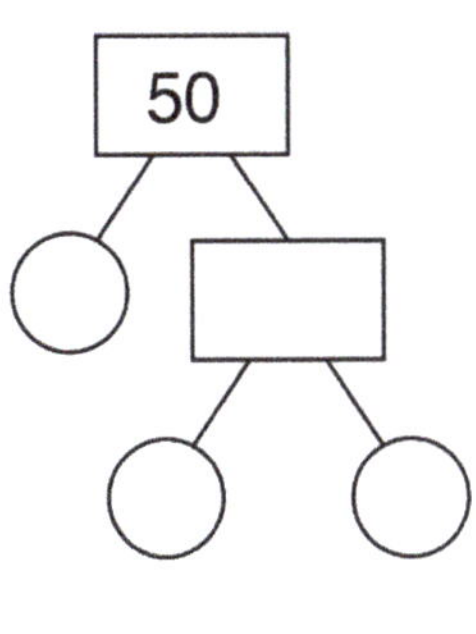

Prime Factors

_ x _ x _ = 50

3) 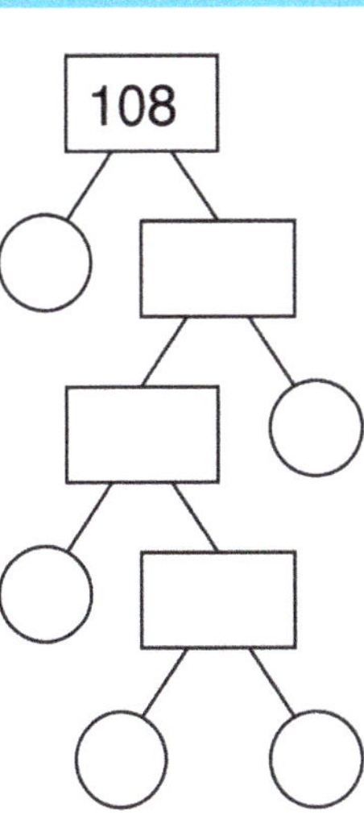

Prime Factors

_ x _ x _ x _ x _ = 108

4) 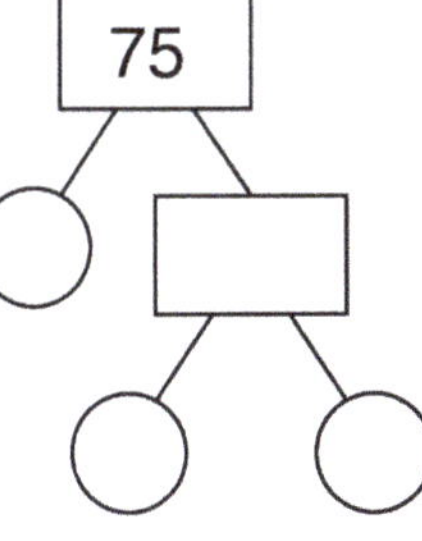

Prime Factors

_ x _ x _ = 75

5) 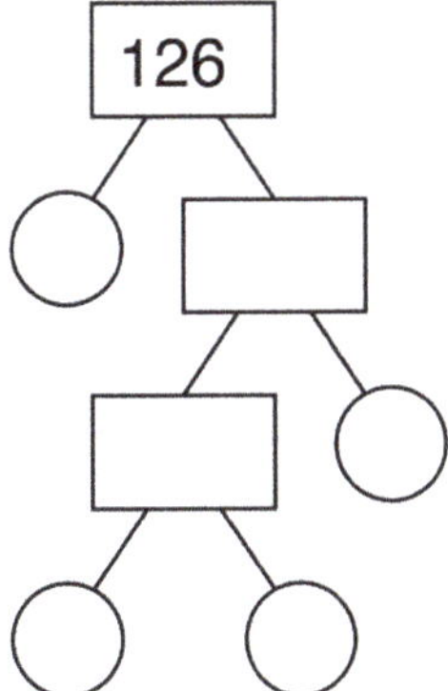

Prime Factors

_ x _ x _ x _ = 126

6) 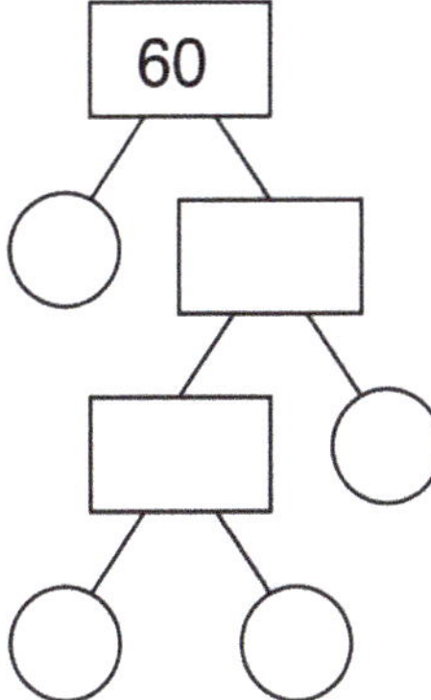

Prime Factors

_ x _ x _ x _ = 60

Find the Prime Factors of the Numbers.

1)

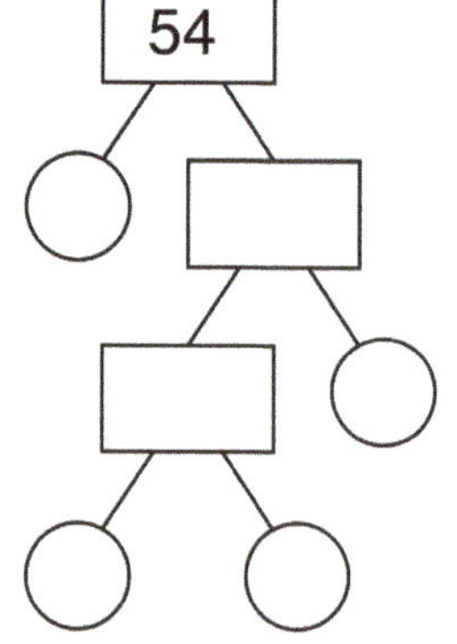

2)

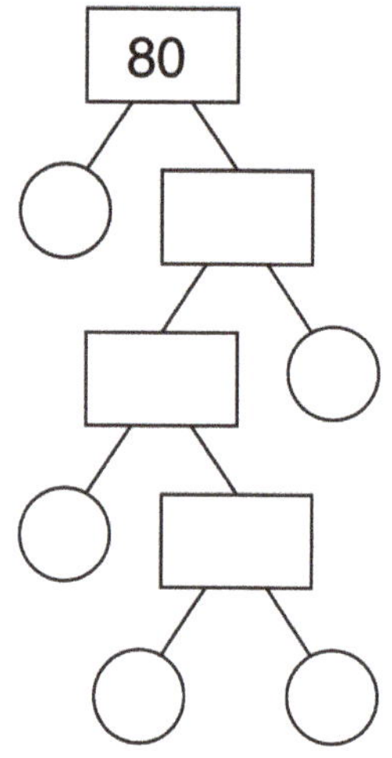

3)

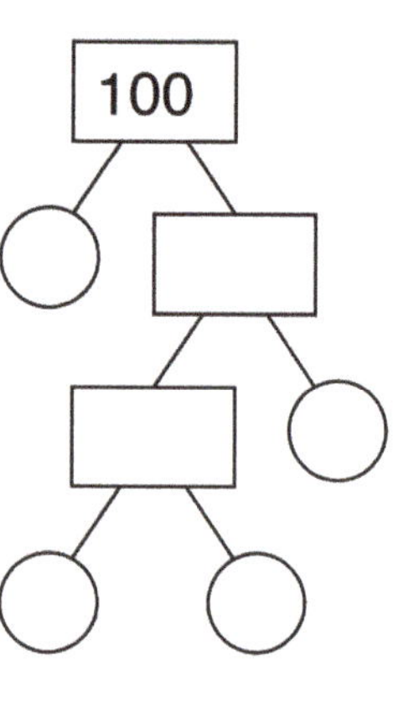

Prime Factors

_ x _ x _ x _ = 54

Prime Factors

_ x _ x _ x _ x _ = 80

Prime Factors

_ x _ x _ x _ = 100

---

4)

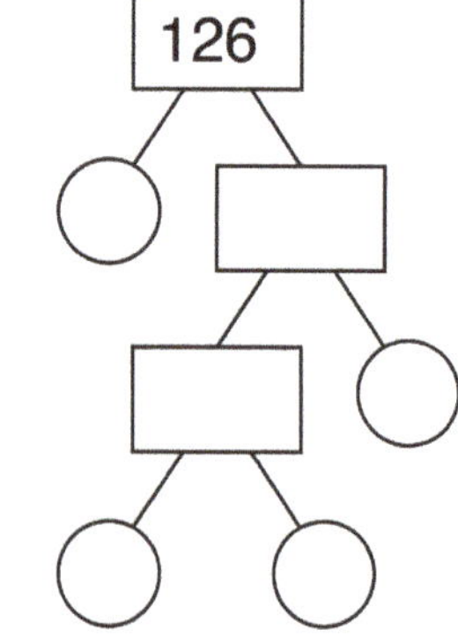

5)

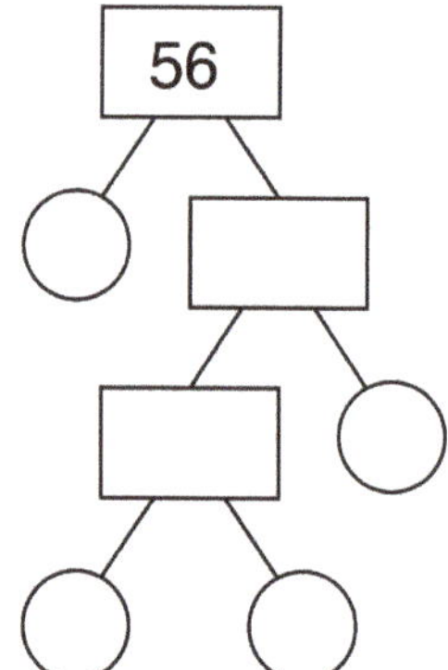

6)

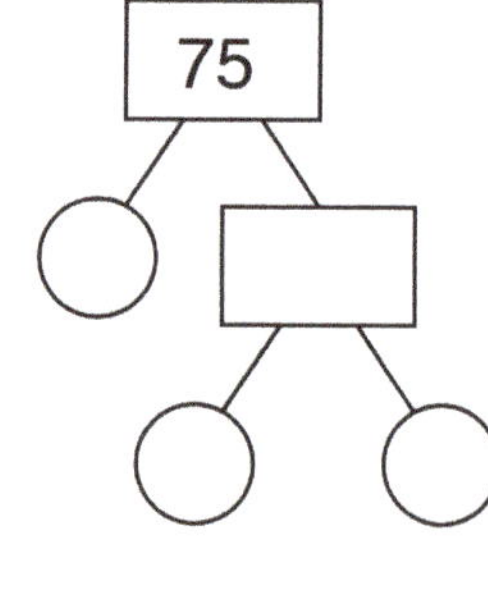

Prime Factors

_ x _ x _ x _ = 126

Prime Factors

_ x _ x _ x _ = 56

Prime Factors

_ x _ x _ = 75

GREATEST
COMMON FACTOR

Find the Greatest Common Factor for each number pair.

1)   5 , 20   _____5_____

2)   20 , 24   _______

3)   40 , 8   _______

4)   30 , 40   _______

5)   6 , 24   _______

6)   20 , 15   _______

7)   8 , 30   _______

8)   60 , 8   _______

Find the Greatest Common Factor for each number pair.

1)   30 , 2   ______

2)   5 , 20   ______

3)   4 , 24   ______

4)   3 , 12   ______

5)   15 , 4   ______

6)   20 , 30   ______

7)   2 , 30   ______

8)   24 , 8   ______

Find the Greatest Common Factor for each number pair.

1) 60 , 4 _______

2) 6 , 12 _______

3) 6 , 5 _______

4) 2 , 24 _______

5) 40 , 15 _______

6) 15 , 12 _______

7) 2 , 12 _______

8) 12 , 3 _______

Find the Greatest Common Factor for each number pair.

1) 6 , 30 _____

2) 20 , 8 _____

3) 8 , 3 _____

4) 8 , 4 _____

5) 20 , 10 _____

6) 3 , 15 _____

7) 10 , 6 _____

8) 3 , 4 _____

Find the Greatest Common Factor for each number pair.

1)   10 , 2   _______

2)   8 , 12   _______

3)   2 , 20   _______

4)   5 , 20   _______

5)   40 , 15   _______

6)   6 , 60   _______

7)   20 , 40   _______

8)   8 , 15   _______

Find the Greatest Common Factor for each number pair.

1)   4 , 3   ______

2)   15 , 60   ______

3)   6 , 5   ______

4)   6 , 12   ______

5)   40 , 4   ______

6)   30 , 5   ______

7)   4 , 15   ______

8)   6 , 24   ______

Find the Greatest Common Factor for each number pair.

1)   20 , 24   ______

2)   20 , 60   ______

3)   20 , 15   ______

4)   40 , 12   ______

5)   15 , 10   ______

6)   2 , 3   ______

7)   8 , 3   ______

8)   10 , 40   ______

Find the Greatest Common Factor for each number pair.

1)　20 , 4　______

2)　3 , 60　______

3)　12 , 40　______

4)　10 , 24　______

5)　5 , 12　______

6)　2 , 30　______

7)　10 , 20　______

8)　4 , 3　______

Find the Greatest Common Factor for each number pair.

1)   8 , 6   ______

2)   12 , 30   ______

3)   40 , 60   ______

4)   24 , 20   ______

5)   40 , 15   ______

6)   12 , 4   ______

7)   15 , 4   ______

8)   4 , 60   ______

Find the Greatest Common Factor for each number pair.

1)   60 , 20   _______

2)   2 , 24   _______

3)   6 , 4   _______

4)   40 , 30   _______

5)   6 , 10   _______

6)   4 , 3   _______

7)   60 , 6   _______

8)   40 , 3   _______

Find the Greatest Common Factor for each number pair.

1)   3 , 8   _______

2)   5 , 10   _______

3)   3 , 10   _______

4)   3 , 6   _______

5)   60 , 3   _______

6)   3 , 24   _______

7)   40 , 10   _______

8)   3 , 6   _______

EXERCISE NO. 32

Find the Greatest Common Factor for each number pair.

1) 6 , 2 ______

2) 3 , 8 ______

3) 3 , 10 ______

4) 12 , 4 ______

5) 12 , 10 ______

6) 60 , 6 ______

7) 8 , 5 ______

8) 6 , 2 ______

Find the Greatest Common Factor for each number pair.

1) 12 , 6 ______

2) 30 , 5 ______

3)   5 , 8 ______

4) 20 , 24 ______

5)   3 , 12 ______

6)   5 , 4 ______

7) 20 , 8 ______

8) 15 , 24 ______

Find the Greatest Common Factor for each number pair.

1)   40 , 3   ______

2)   15 , 6   ______

3)   30 , 4   ______

4)   24 , 10   ______

5)   10 , 4   ______

6)   40 , 20   ______

7)   24 , 60   ______

8)   5 , 12   ______

Find the Greatest Common Factor for each number pair.

1) 60 , 15 ______

2) 8 , 2 ______

3) 30 , 2 ______

4) 6 , 40 ______

5) 15 , 60 ______

6) 4 , 24 ______

7) 5 , 20 ______

8) 4 , 12 ______

LIST ALL FACTORS OF A NUMBER

EXERCISE NO. 36

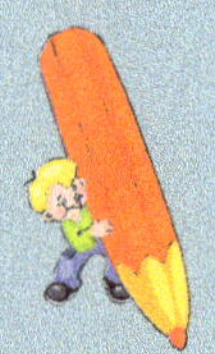

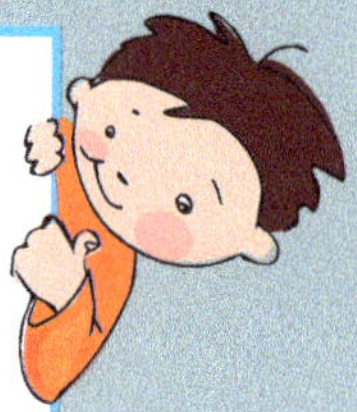

List all of the factors for each number.

1) 10 1, 2, 5, 10

2) 12 ____________________

3) 70 ____________________

4) 65 ____________________

5) 30 ____________________

6) 25 ____________________

7) 64 ____________________

8) 24 ____________________

9) 28 ____________________

10) 60 ____________________

EXERCISE NO. 37

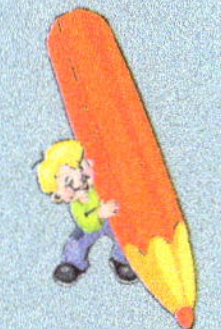

List all of the factors for each number.

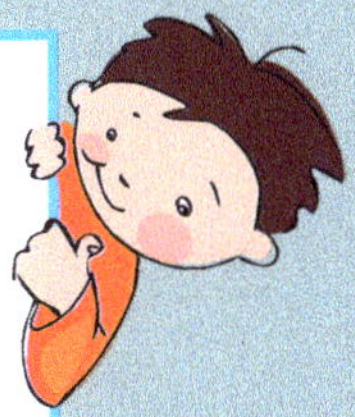

1) 21 ______________________________

2) 50 ______________________________

3) 26 ______________________________

4) 69 ______________________________

5) 28 ______________________________

6) 39 ______________________________

7) 56 ______________________________

8) 60 ______________________________

9) 74 ______________________________

10) 38 ______________________________

EXERCISE NO. 38

List all of the factors for each number.

1)   12   ____

2)   52   ____

3)   72   ____

4)   40   ____

5)   65   ____

6)   68   ____

7)   78   ____

8)   14   ____

9)   69   ____

10)   76   ____

EXERCISE NO. 39

List all of the factors for each number.

1)　25 _______________________________________

2)　26 _______________________________________

3)　21 _______________________________________

4)　35 _______________________________________

5)　58 _______________________________________

6)　27 _______________________________________

7)　60 _______________________________________

8)　48 _______________________________________

9)　12 _______________________________________

10)　28 _______________________________________

EXERCISE NO. 40

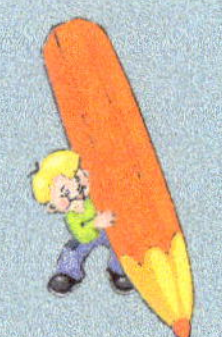

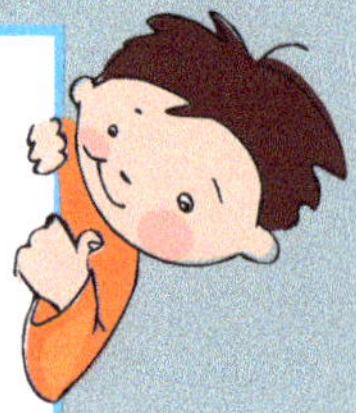

List all of the factors for each number.

1) 18 ______________________________

2) 72 ______________________________

3) 55 ______________________________

4) 49 ______________________________

5) 32 ______________________________

6) 69 ______________________________

7) 39 ______________________________

8) 54 ______________________________

9) 70 ______________________________

10) 65 ______________________________

EXERCISE NO. 41

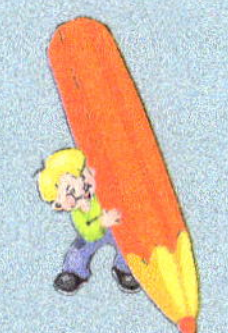

List all of the factors for each number.

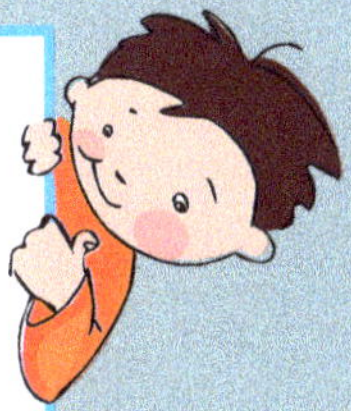

1) 46 ______________________________

2) 40 ______________________________

3) 69 ______________________________

4) 64 ______________________________

5) 65 ______________________________

6) 63 ______________________________

7) 25 ______________________________

8) 77 ______________________________

9) 18 ______________________________

10) 74 ______________________________

EXERCISE NO. 42

List all of the factors for each number.

1)   36 ______________________________________

2)   56 ______________________________________

3)   45 ______________________________________

4)   62 ______________________________________

5)   48 ______________________________________

6)   77 ______________________________________

7)   42 ______________________________________

8)   74 ______________________________________

9)   12 ______________________________________

10)   34 ______________________________________

Find the Prime Factors of the Numbers.

1) 15 ____

2) 39 ____

3) 60 ____

4) 36 ____

5) 76 ____

6) 62 ____

7) 68 ____

8) 38 ____

9) 70 ____

10) 77 ____

EXERCISE NO. 44

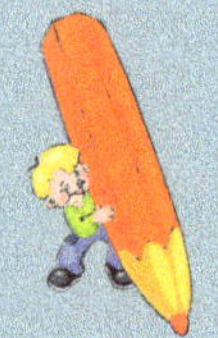

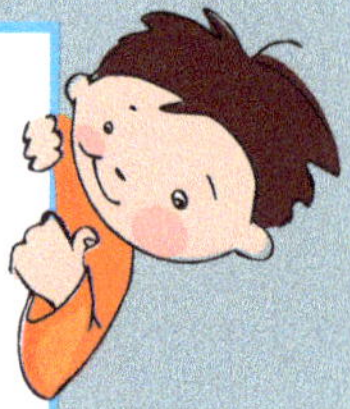

List all of the factors for each number.

1) 57 ____________________

2) 32 ____________________

3) 66 ____________________

4) 22 ____________________

5) 63 ____________________

6) 49 ____________________

7) 24 ____________________

8) 62 ____________________

9) 45 ____________________

10) 20 ____________________

EXERCISE NO. 1

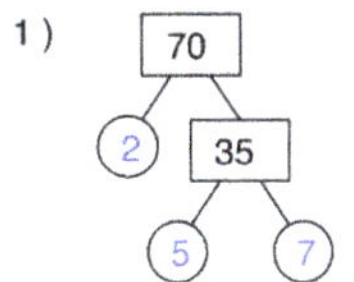  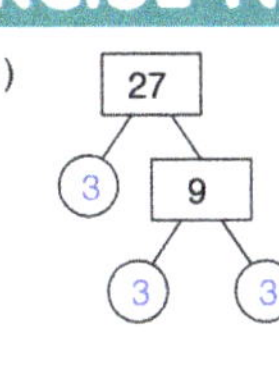 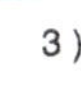 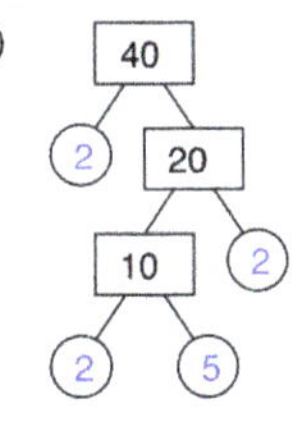

1)

Factors
2 x 5 x 7 = 70

2)

Factors
3 x 3 x 3 = 27

3)

Factors
2 x 2 x 2 x 5 = 40

4)

Factors
2 x 5 x 5 = 50

5)

Factors
2 x 2 x 2 x 2 = 16

6)

Factors
2 x 2 x 17 = 68

EXERCISE NO. 2

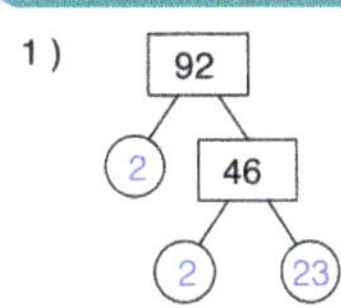 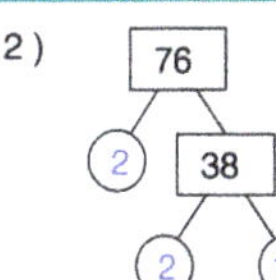 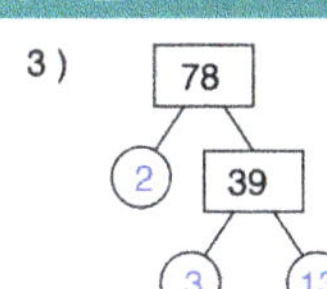

1)

Factors
2 x 2 x 23 = 92

2)

Factors
2 x 2 x 19 = 76

3)

Factors
2 x 3 x 13 = 78

4)

Factors
2 x 5 x 5 = 50

5)

Factors
2 x 2 x 2 x 2 = 16

6)

Factors
2 x 3 x 11 = 66

EXERCISE NO. 3

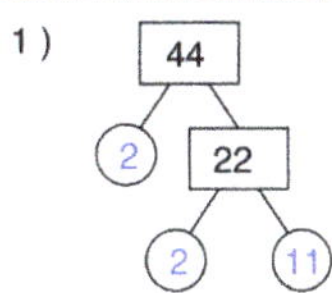  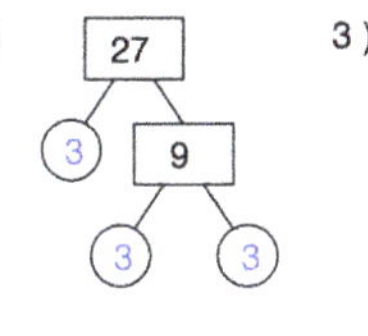 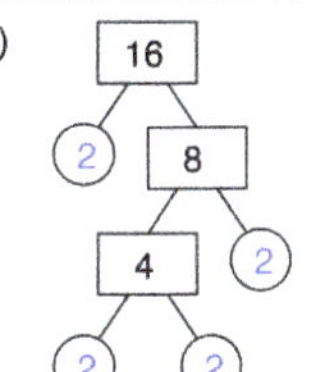  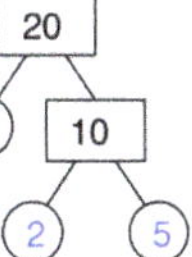 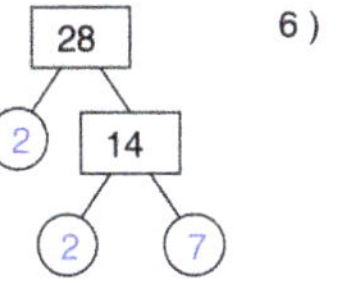 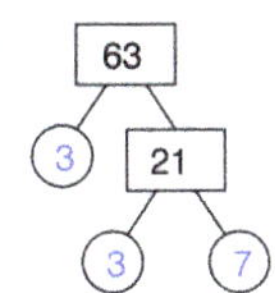

1)

Factors
2 x 2 x 11 = 44

2)

Factors
3 x 3 x 3 = 27

3)

Factors
2 x 2 x 2 x 2 = 16

4)

Factors
2 x 2 x 5 = 20

5)

Factors
2 x 2 x 7 = 28

6)

Factors
3 x 3 x 7 = 63

EXERCISE NO. 4

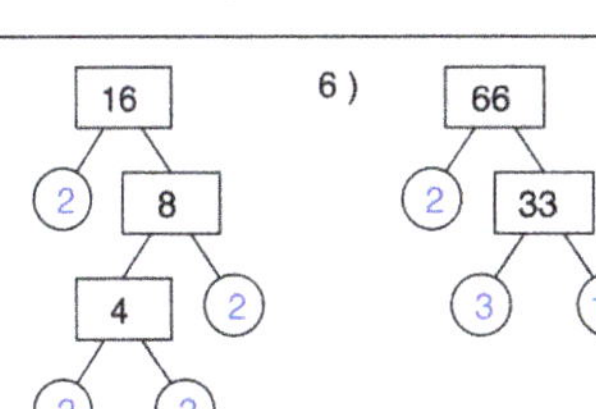 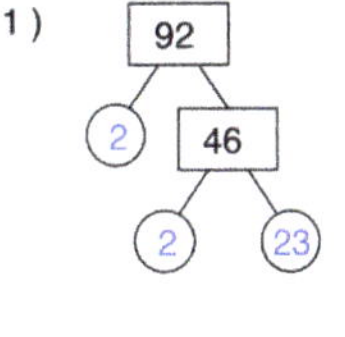 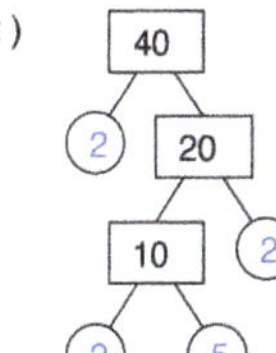 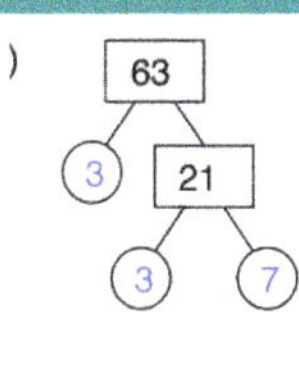 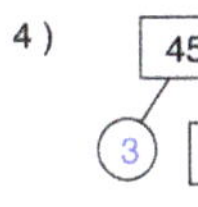 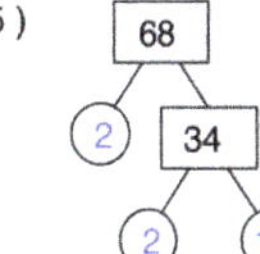 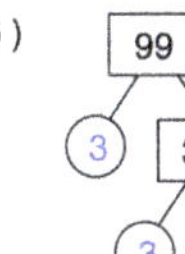

1)

Factors
2 x 2 x 23 = 92

2)

Factors
2 x 2 x 2 x 5 = 40

3)

Factors
3 x 3 x 7 = 63

4)

Factors
3 x 3 x 5 = 45

5)

Factors
2 x 2 x 17 = 68

6)

Factors
3 x 3 x 11 = 99

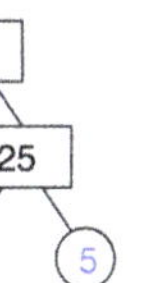 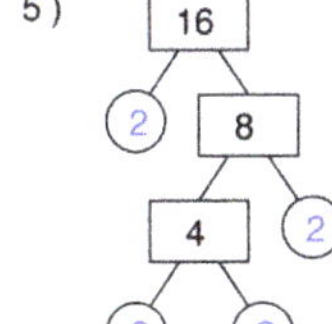  

EXERCISE NO. 5

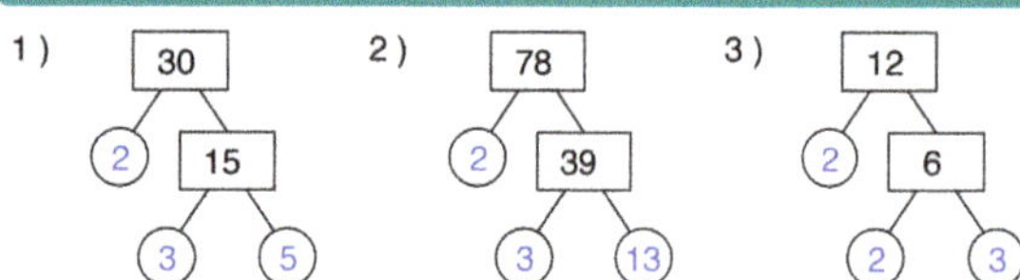

Factors
2 x 3 x 5 = 30

Factors
2 x 3 x 13 = 78

Factors
2 x 2 x 3 = 12

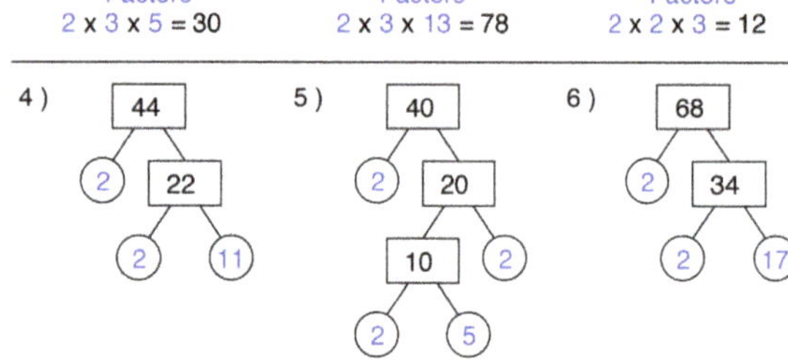

Factors
2 x 2 x 11 = 44

Factors
2 x 2 x 2 x 5 = 40

Factors
2 x 2 x 17 = 68

EXERCISE NO. 6

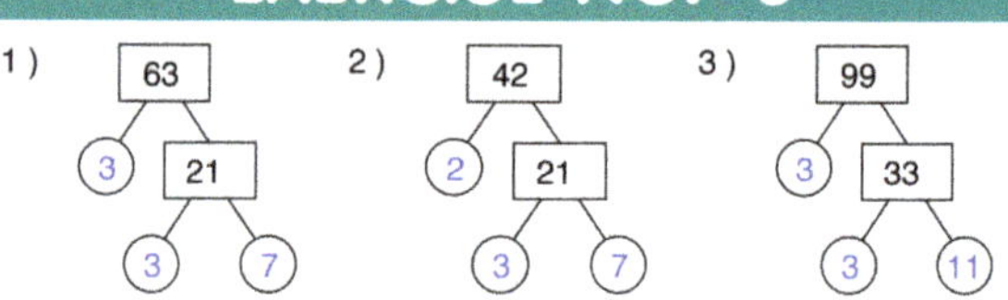

Factors
3 x 3 x 7 = 63

Factors
2 x 3 x 7 = 42

Factors
3 x 3 x 11 = 99

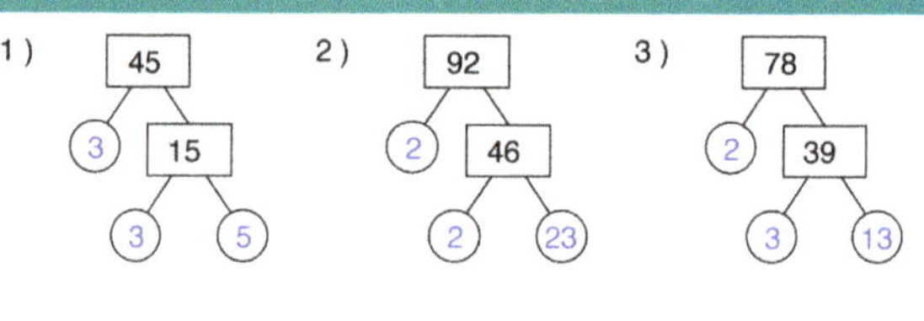

Factors
2 x 5 x 5 = 50

Factors
2 x 3 x 5 = 30

Factors
2 x 3 x 11 = 66

EXERCISE NO. 7

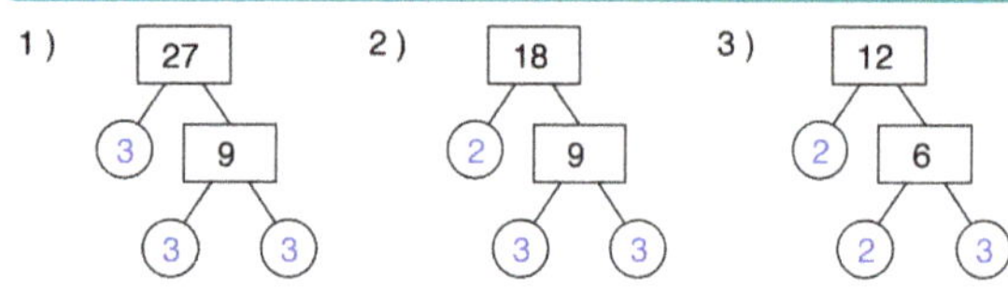

Factors
3 x 3 x 3 = 27

Factors
2 x 3 x 3 = 18

Factors
2 x 2 x 3 = 12

Factors
3 x 3 x 11 = 99

Factors
2 x 3 x 11 = 66

Factors
2 x 2 x 7 = 28

EXERCISE NO. 8

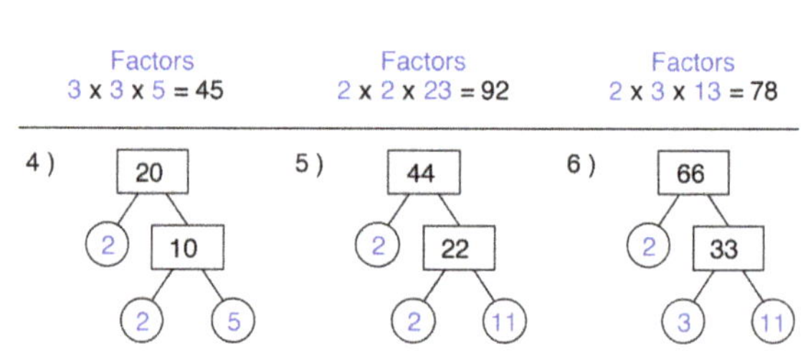

Factors
3 x 3 x 5 = 45

Factors
2 x 2 x 23 = 92

Factors
2 x 3 x 13 = 78

Factors
2 x 2 x 5 = 20

Factors
2 x 2 x 11 = 44

Factors
2 x 3 x 11 = 66

EXERCISE NO. 9

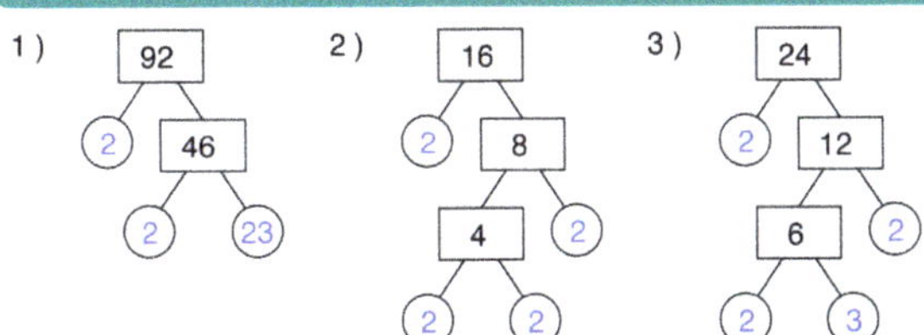

1) 92 → 2, 46 → 2, 23
2) 16 → 2, 8 → 4, 2 → 2, 2
3) 24 → 2, 12 → 6, 2 → 2, 3

Factors
2 x 2 x 23 = 92

Factors
2 x 2 x 2 x 2 = 16

Factors
2 x 2 x 2 x 3 = 24

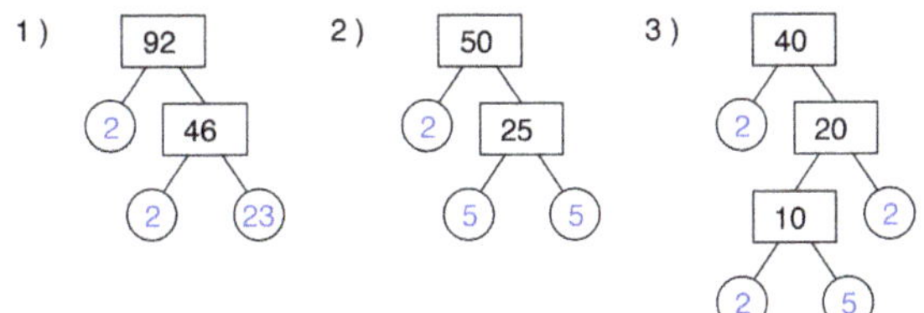

4) 45 → 3, 15 → 3, 5
5) 12 → 2, 6 → 2, 3
6) 30 → 2, 15 → 3, 5

Factors
3 x 3 x 5 = 45

Factors
2 x 2 x 3 = 12

Factors
2 x 3 x 5 = 30

EXERCISE NO. 10

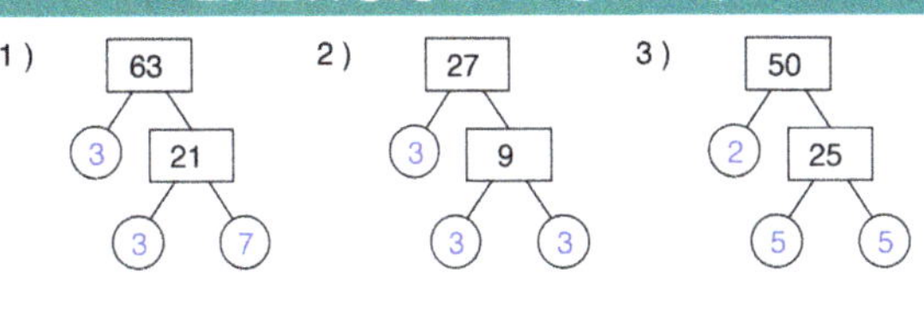

1) 63 → 3, 21 → 3, 7
2) 27 → 3, 9 → 3, 3
3) 50 → 2, 25 → 5, 5

Factors
3 x 3 x 7 = 63

Factors
3 x 3 x 3 = 27

Factors
2 x 5 x 5 = 50

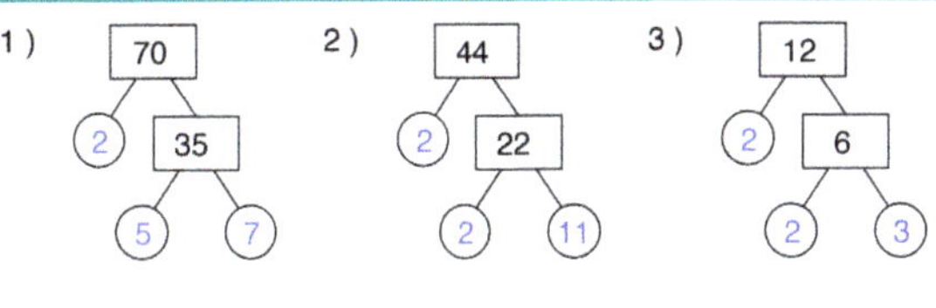

4) 44 → 2, 22 → 2, 11
5) 40 → 2, 20 → 10, 2 → 2, 5
6) 66 → 2, 33 → 3, 11

Factors
2 x 2 x 11 = 44

Factors
2 x 2 x 2 x 5 = 40

Factors
2 x 3 x 11 = 66

EXERCISE NO. 11

1) 92 → 2, 46 → 2, 23
2) 50 → 2, 25 → 5, 5
3) 40 → 2, 20 → 10, 2 → 2, 5

Factors
2 x 2 x 23 = 92

Factors
2 x 5 x 5 = 50

Factors
2 x 2 x 2 x 5 = 40

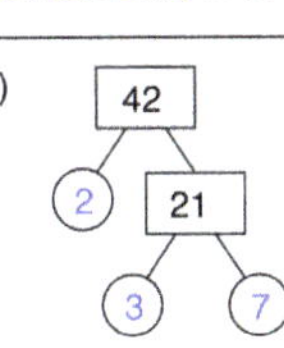

4) 20 → 2, 10 → 2, 5
5) 18 → 2, 9 → 3, 3
6) 42 → 2, 21 → 3, 7

Factors
2 x 2 x 5 = 20

Factors
2 x 3 x 3 = 18

Factors
2 x 3 x 7 = 42

EXERCISE NO. 12

1) 70 → 2, 35 → 5, 7
2) 44 → 2, 22 → 2, 11
3) 12 → 2, 6 → 2, 3

Factors
2 x 5 x 7 = 70

Factors
2 x 2 x 11 = 44

Factors
2 x 2 x 3 = 12

4) 20 → 2, 10 → 2, 5
5) 68 → 2, 34 → 2, 17
6) 63 → 3, 21 → 3, 7

Factors
2 x 2 x 5 = 20

Factors
2 x 2 x 17 = 68

Factors
3 x 3 x 7 = 63

EXERCISE NO. 13

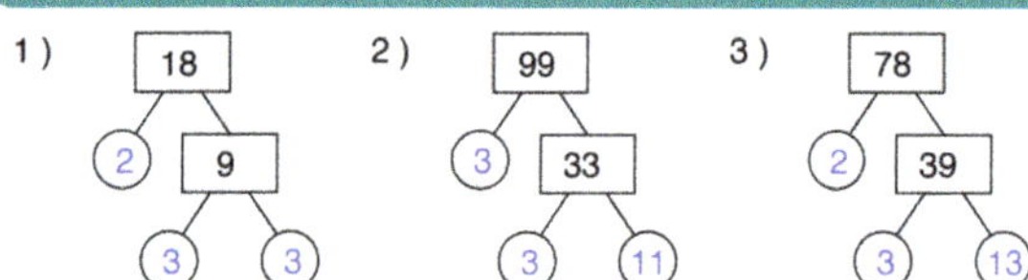

1) 18

2) 99

3) 78

Factors
2 x 3 x 3 = 18

Factors
3 x 3 x 11 = 99

Factors
2 x 3 x 13 = 78

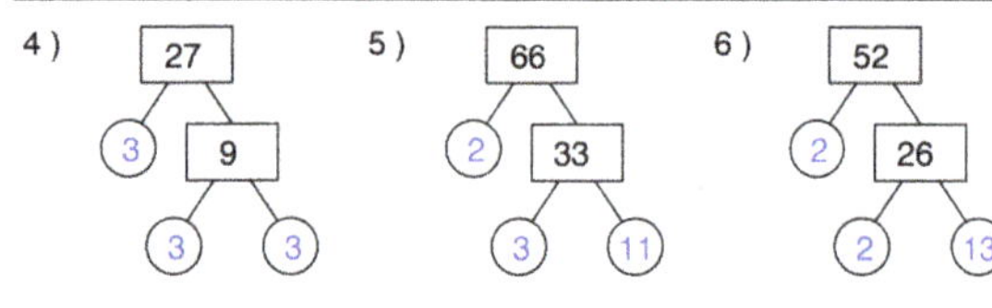

4) 27

5) 66

6) 52

Factors
3 x 3 x 3 = 27

Factors
2 x 3 x 11 = 66

Factors
2 x 2 x 13 = 52

EXERCISE NO. 15

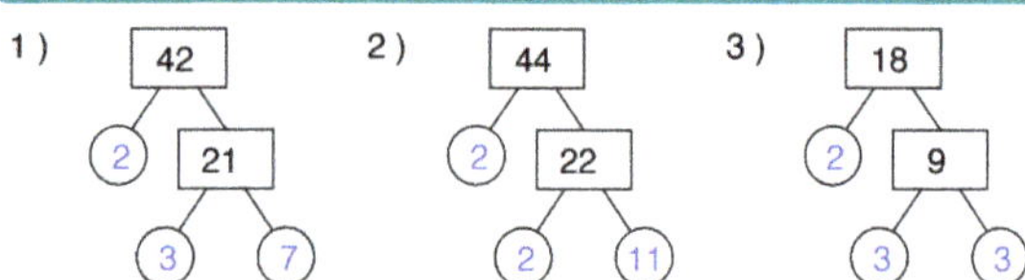

1) 42

2) 44

3) 18

Factors
2 x 3 x 7 = 42

Factors
2 x 2 x 11 = 44

Factors
2 x 3 x 3 = 18

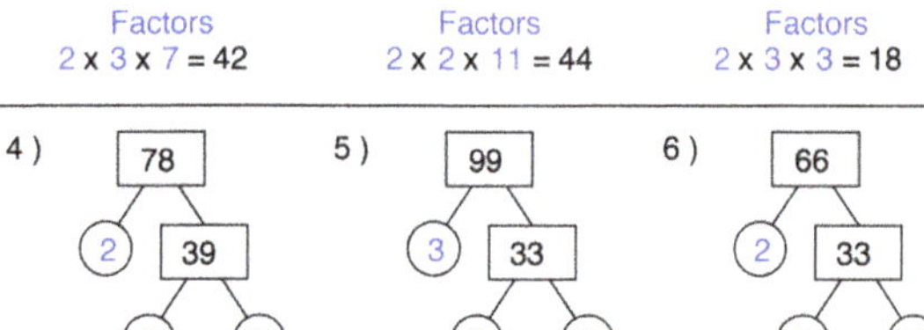

4) 78

5) 99

6) 66

Factors
2 x 3 x 13 = 78

Factors
3 x 3 x 11 = 99

Factors
2 x 3 x 11 = 66

EXERCISE NO. 14

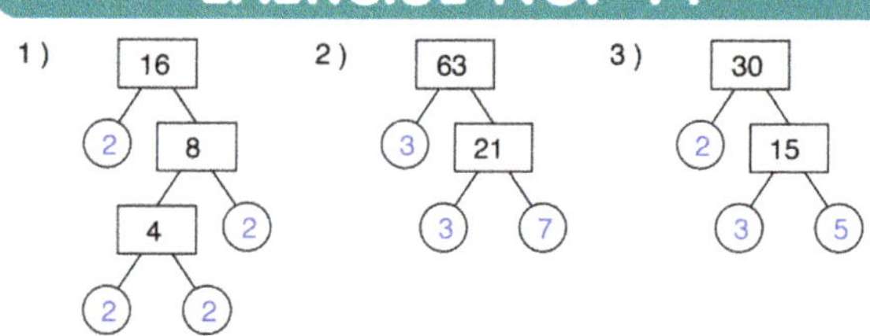

1) 16

2) 63

3) 30

Factors
2 x 2 x 2 x 2 = 16

Factors
3 x 3 x 7 = 63

Factors
2 x 3 x 5 = 30

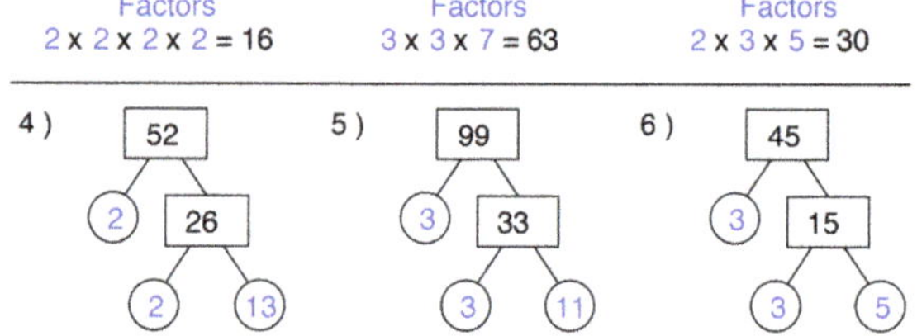

4) 52

5) 99

6) 45

Factors
2 x 2 x 13 = 52

Factors
3 x 3 x 11 = 99

Factors
3 x 3 x 5 = 45

EXERCISE NO. 16

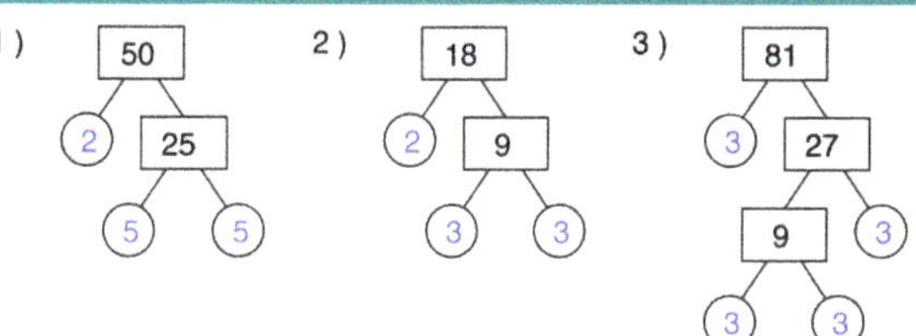

1) 50

2) 18

3) 81

Factors
2 x 5 x 5 = 50

Factors
2 x 3 x 3 = 18

Factors
3 x 3 x 3 x 3 = 81

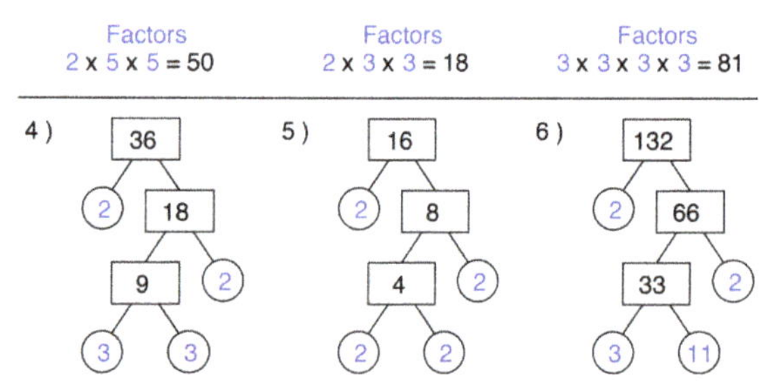

4) 36

5) 16

6) 132

Factors
2 x 2 x 3 x 3 = 36

Factors
2 x 2 x 2 x 2 = 16

Factors
2 x 2 x 3 x 11 = 132

EXERCISE NO. 17

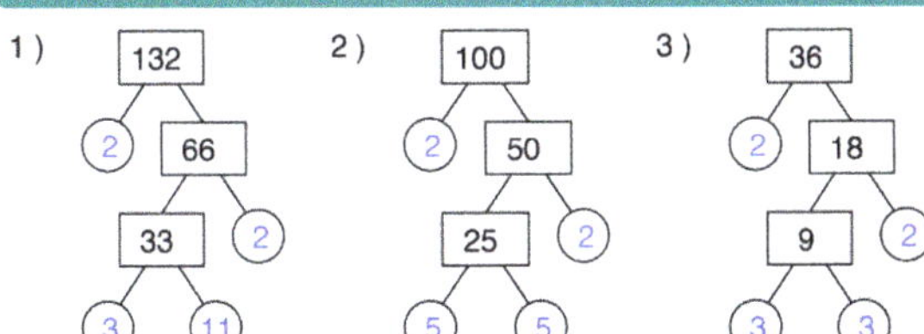

1)
2)
3)

Factors
2 x 2 x 3 x 11 = 132

Factors
2 x 2 x 5 x 5 = 100

Factors
2 x 2 x 3 x 3 = 36

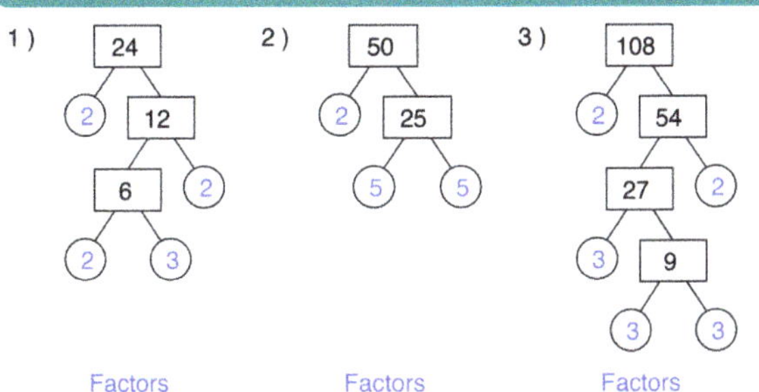

4)
5)
6)

Factors
2 x 2 x 2 x 2 x 2 = 32

Factors
2 x 2 x 2 x 7 = 56

Factors
3 x 3 x 3 x 3 = 81

EXERCISE NO. 18

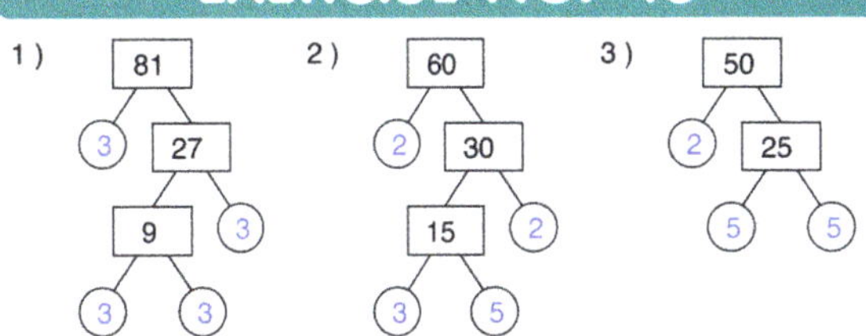

1)
2)
3)

Factors
3 x 3 x 3 x 3 = 81

Factors
2 x 2 x 3 x 5 = 60

Factors
2 x 5 x 5 = 50

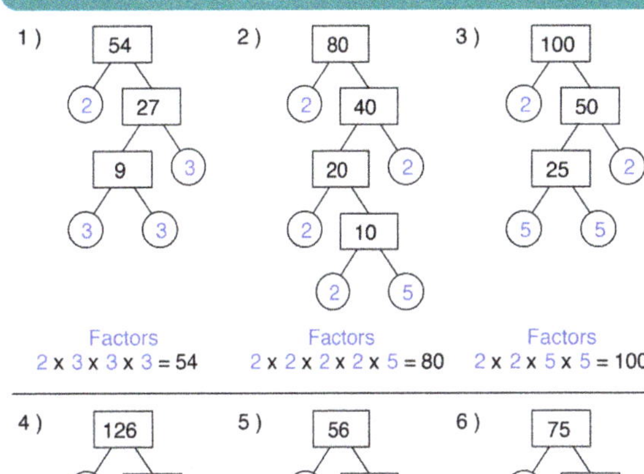

4)
5)
6)

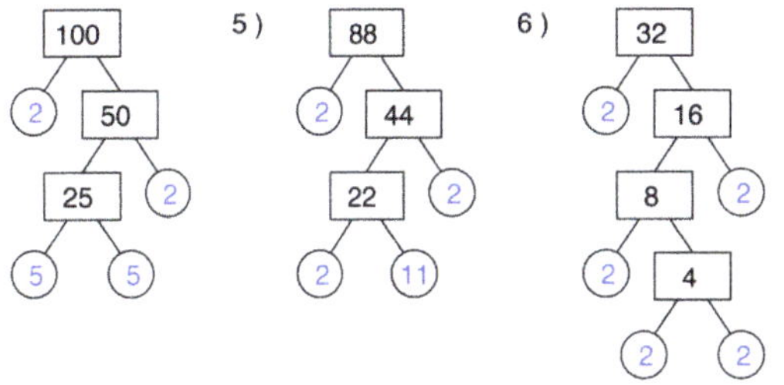

Factors
2 x 2 x 5 x 5 = 100

Factors
2 x 2 x 2 x 11 = 88

Factors
2 x 2 x 2 x 2 x 2 = 32

EXERCISE NO. 19

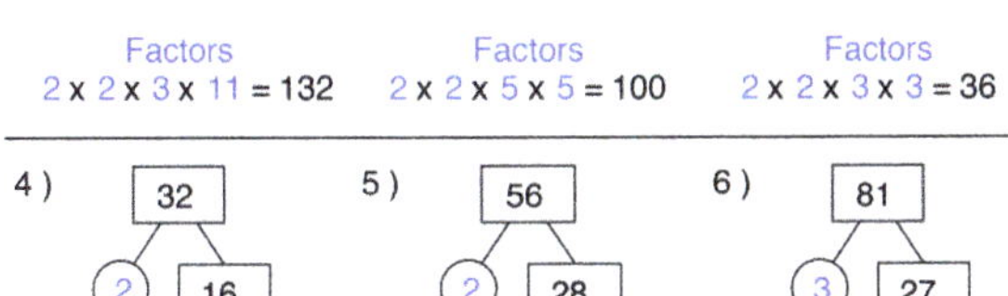

1)
2)
3)

Factors
2 x 2 x 2 x 3 = 24

Factors
2 x 5 x 5 = 50

Factors
2 x 2 x 3 x 3 x 3 = 108

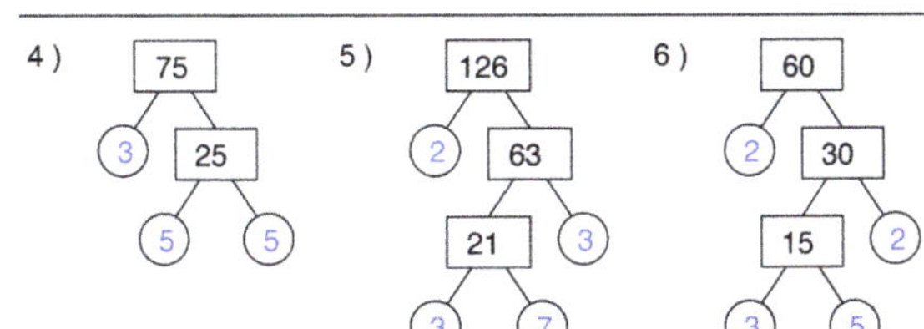

4)
5)
6)

Factors
3 x 5 x 5 = 75

Factors
2 x 3 x 3 x 7 = 126

Factors
2 x 2 x 3 x 5 = 60

EXERCISE NO. 20

1)
2)
3)

Factors
2 x 3 x 3 x 3 = 54

Factors
2 x 2 x 2 x 2 x 5 = 80

Factors
2 x 2 x 5 x 5 = 100

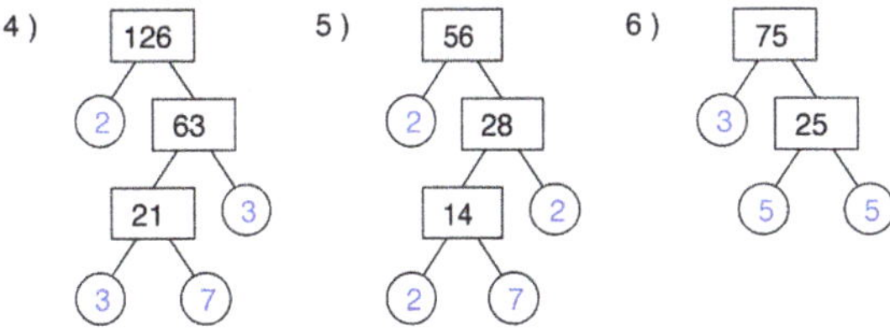

4)
5)
6)

Factors
2 x 3 x 3 x 7 = 126

Factors
2 x 2 x 2 x 7 = 56

Factors
3 x 5 x 5 = 75

EXERCISE NO. 21

1) 5 , 20   5
2) 20 , 24   4
3) 40 , 8   8
4) 30 , 40   10
5) 6 , 24   6
6) 20 , 15   5
7) 8 , 30   2
8) 60 , 8   4

EXERCISE NO. 22

1) 30 , 2   2
2) 5 , 20   5
3) 4 , 24   4
4) 3 , 12   3
5) 15 , 4   1
6) 20 , 30   10
7) 2 , 30   2
8) 24 , 8   8

EXERCISE NO. 23

1) 60 , 4   4
2) 6 , 12   6
3) 6 , 5   1
4) 2 , 24   2
5) 40 , 15   5
6) 15 , 12   3
7) 2 , 12   2
8) 12 , 3   3

EXERCISE NO. 24

1) 6 , 30   6
2) 20 , 8   4
3) 8 , 3   1
4) 8 , 4   4
5) 20 , 10   10
6) 3 , 15   3
7) 10 , 6   2
8) 3 , 4   1

EXERCISE NO. 25

1) 10 , 2   2

2) 8 , 12   4

3) 2 , 20   2

4) 5 , 20   5

5) 40 , 15   5

6) 6 , 60   6

7) 20 , 40   20

8) 8 , 15   1

EXERCISE NO. 26

1) 4 , 3   1

2) 15 , 60   15

3) 6 , 5   1

4) 6 , 12   6

5) 40 , 4   4

6) 30 , 5   5

7) 4 , 15   1

8) 6 , 24   6

EXERCISE NO. 27

1) 20 , 24   4

2) 20 , 60   20

3) 20 , 15   5

4) 40 , 12   4

5) 15 , 10   5

6) 2 , 3   1

7) 8 , 3   1

8) 10 , 40   10

EXERCISE NO. 28

1) 20 , 4   4

2) 3 , 60   3

3) 12 , 40   4

4) 10 , 24   2

5) 5 , 12   1

6) 2 , 30   2

7) 10 , 20   10

8) 4 , 3   1

EXERCISE NO. 29

1)   8 , 6 _ 2 _
2)   12 , 30 _ 6 _
3)   40 , 60 _ 20 _
4)   24 , 20 _ 4 _
5)   40 , 15 _ 5 _
6)   12 , 4 _ 4 _
7)   15 , 4 _ 1 _
8)   4 , 60 _ 4 _

EXERCISE NO. 30

1)   60 , 20 _ 20 _
2)   2 , 24 _ 2 _
3)   6 , 4 _ 2 _
4)   40 , 30 _ 10 _
5)   6 , 10 _ 2 _
6)   4 , 3 _ 1 _
7)   60 , 6 _ 6 _
8)   40 , 3 _ 1 _

EXERCISE NO. 31

1)   3 , 8 _ 24 _
2)   5 , 10 _ 10 _
3)   3 , 10 _ 30 _
4)   3 , 6 _ 6 _
5)   60 , 3 _ 60 _
6)   3 , 24 _ 24 _
7)   40 , 10 _ 40 _
8)   3 , 6 _ 6 _

EXERCISE NO. 32

1)   6 , 2 _ 6 _
2)   3 , 8 _ 24 _
3)   3 , 10 _ 30 _
4)   12 , 4 _ 12 _
5)   12 , 10 _ 60 _
6)   60 , 6 _ 60 _
7)   8 , 5 _ 40 _
8)   6 , 2 _ 6 _

EXERCISE NO. 33

1) 12 , 6 __12__

2) 30 , 5 __30__

3) 5 , 8 __40__

4) 20 , 24 __120__

5) 3 , 12 __12__

6) 5 , 4 __20__

7) 20 , 8 __40__

8) 15 , 24 __120__

EXERCISE NO. 34

1) 40 , 3 __120__

2) 15 , 6 __30__

3) 30 , 4 __60__

4) 24 , 10 __120__

5) 10 , 4 __20__

6) 40 , 20 __40__

7) 24 , 60 __120__

8) 5 , 12 __60__

EXERCISE NO. 35

1) 60 , 15 __60__

2) 8 , 2 __8__

3) 30 , 2 __30__

4) 6 , 40 __120__

5) 15 , 60 __60__

6) 4 , 24 __24__

7) 5 , 20 __20__

8) 4 , 12 __12__

EXERCISE NO. 36

1) 10 __1 , 2 , 5 , 10__

2) 12 __1 , 2 , 3 , 4 , 6 , 12__

3) 70 __1 , 2 , 5 , 7 , 10, 14, 35, 70__

4) 65 __1 , 5 , 13, 65__

5) 30 __1 , 2 , 3 , 5 , 6 , 10, 15, 30__

6) 25 __1 , 5 , 25__

7) 64 __1 , 2 , 4 , 8 , 16, 32, 64__

8) 24 __1 , 2 , 3 , 4 , 6 , 8 , 12, 24__

9) 28 __1 , 2 , 4 , 7 , 14, 28__

10) 60 __1 , 2 , 3 , 4 , 5 , 6 , 10, 12, 15, 20, 30, 60__

EXERCISE NO. 37

1) 21   1 , 3 , 7 , 21
2) 50   1 , 2 , 5 , 10, 25, 50
3) 26   1 , 2 , 13, 26
4) 69   1 , 3 , 23, 69
5) 28   1 , 2 , 4 , 7 , 14, 28
6) 39   1 , 3 , 13, 39
7) 56   1 , 2 , 4 , 7 , 8 , 14, 28, 56
8) 60   1 , 2 , 3 , 4 , 5 , 6 , 10, 12, 15, 20, 30, 60
9) 74   1 , 2 , 37, 74
10) 38   1 , 2 , 19, 38

EXERCISE NO. 38

1) 12   1 , 2 , 3 , 4 , 6 , 12
2) 52   1 , 2 , 4 , 13, 26, 52
3) 72   1 , 2 , 3 , 4 , 6 , 8 , 9 , 12, 18, 24, 36, 72
4) 40   1 , 2 , 4 , 5 , 8 , 10, 20, 40
5) 65   1 , 5 , 13, 65
6) 68   1 , 2 , 4 , 17, 34, 68
7) 78   1 , 2 , 3 , 6 , 13, 26, 39, 78
8) 14   1 , 2 , 7 , 14
9) 69   1 , 3 , 23, 69
10) 76   1 , 2 , 4 , 19, 38, 76

EXERCISE NO. 39

1) 25   1 , 5 , 25
2) 26   1 , 2 , 13, 26
3) 21   1 , 3 , 7 , 21
4) 35   1 , 5 , 7 , 35
5) 58   1 , 2 , 29, 58
6) 27   1 , 3 , 9 , 27
7) 60   1 , 2 , 3 , 4 , 5 , 6 , 10, 12, 15, 20, 30, 60
8) 48   1 , 2 , 3 , 4 , 6 , 8 , 12, 16, 24, 48
9) 12   1 , 2 , 3 , 4 , 6 , 12
10) 28   1 , 2 , 4 , 7 , 14, 28

EXERCISE NO. 40

1) 18   1 , 2 , 3 , 6 , 9 , 18
2) 72   1 , 2 , 3 , 4 , 6 , 8 , 9 , 12, 18, 24, 36, 72
3) 55   1 , 5 , 11, 55
4) 49   1 , 7 , 49
5) 32   1 , 2 , 4 , 8 , 16, 32
6) 69   1 , 3 , 23, 69
7) 39   1 , 3 , 13, 39
8) 54   1 , 2 , 3 , 6 , 9 , 18, 27, 54
9) 70   1 , 2 , 5 , 7 , 10, 14, 35, 70
10) 65   1 , 5 , 13, 65

<table>
<tr><td>

EXERCISE NO. 41

1) 46   1 , 2 , 23, 46

2) 40   1 , 2 , 4 , 5 , 8 , 10, 20, 40

3) 69   1 , 3 , 23, 69

4) 64   1 , 2 , 4 , 8 , 16, 32, 64

5) 65   1 , 5 , 13, 65

6) 63   1 , 3 , 7 , 9 , 21, 63

7) 25   1 , 5 , 25

8) 77   1 , 7 , 11, 77

9) 18   1 , 2 , 3 , 6 , 9 , 18

10) 74   1 , 2 , 37, 74

</td><td>

EXERCISE NO. 42

1) 36   1 , 2 , 3 , 4 , 6 , 9 , 12, 18, 36

2) 56   1 , 2 , 4 , 7 , 8 , 14, 28, 56

3) 45   1 , 3 , 5 , 9 , 15, 45

4) 62   1 , 2 , 31, 62

5) 48   1 , 2 , 3 , 4 , 6 , 8 , 12, 16, 24, 48

6) 77   1 , 7 , 11, 77

7) 42   1 , 2 , 3 , 6 , 7 , 14, 21, 42

8) 74   1 , 2 , 37, 74

9) 12   1 , 2 , 3 , 4 , 6 , 12

10) 34   1 , 2 , 17, 34

</td></tr>
<tr><td>

EXERCISE NO. 43

1) 15   1 , 3 , 5 , 15

2) 39   1 , 3 , 13, 39

3) 60   1 , 2 , 3 , 4 , 5 , 6 , 10, 12, 15, 20, 30, 60

4) 36   1 , 2 , 3 , 4 , 6 , 9 , 12, 18, 36

5) 76   1 , 2 , 4 , 19, 38, 76

6) 62   1 , 2 , 31, 62

7) 68   1 , 2 , 4 , 17, 34, 68

8) 38   1 , 2 , 19, 38

9) 70   1 , 2 , 5 , 7 , 10, 14, 35, 70

10) 77   1 , 7 , 11, 77

</td><td>

EXERCISE NO. 44

1) 57   1 , 3 , 19, 57

2) 32   1 , 2 , 4 , 8 , 16, 32

3) 66   1 , 2 , 3 , 6 , 11, 22, 33, 66

4) 22   1 , 2 , 11, 22

5) 63   1 , 3 , 7 , 9 , 21, 63

6) 49   1 , 7 , 49

7) 24   1 , 2 , 3 , 4 , 6 , 8 , 12, 24

8) 62   1 , 2 , 31, 62

9) 45   1 , 3 , 5 , 9 , 15, 45

10) 20   1 , 2 , 4 , 5 , 10, 20

</td></tr>
</table>

Visit
BABY PROFESSOR
EDUCATION KIDS
www.BabyProfessorBooks.com
to download Free Baby Professor eBooks
and view our catalog of new and exciting
Children's Books